Gossiping
Jesus

Gossiping Jesus

The Oral Processing of Jesus in John's Gospel

JOHN W. DANIELS JR.

◆PICKWICK *Publications* • Eugene, Oregon

GOSSIPING JESUS
The Oral Processing of Jesus in John's Gospel

Copyright © 2013 John W. Daniels Jr. All rights reserved. Except for brief quotations in critical publications or reviews, no part of this book may be reproduced in any manner without prior written permission from the publisher. Write: Permissions, Wipf and Stock Publishers, 199 W. 8th Ave., Suite 3, Eugene, OR 97401.

Pickwick Publications
An Imprint of Wipf and Stock Publishers
199 W. 8th Ave., Suite 3
Eugene, OR 97401

www.wipfandstock.com

ISBN 13: 978-1-61097-480-6

Cataloguing-in-Publication data:

Daniels, John W., Jr.

Gossiping Jesus : the oral processing of Jesus in John's gospel / John W. Daniels Jr.

viii + 118 pp. ; 23 cm. Includes bibliographical references.

ISBN 13: 978-1-61097-480-6

1. Bible. John—Social scientific criticism. 2. Jesus Christ—Person and offices. 3. Gossip. I. Title.

BS2615.52 D35 2013

Manufactured in the U.S.A.

Scripture quotations, unless otherwise indicated, are from the New Revised Standard Version Bible, copyright © 1989, by the Division of Christian Education of the National Council of Churches of Christ in the United States of America.

Scripture transliterations, unless otherwise indicated, are of the twenty-seventh edition of Novum Testamentum Graece, copyright © 1993, by the American Bible Society.

Contents

Acknowledgments   vii

1 Constructing Gossip and Jesus   1

2 Gossip in Jesus' Social World   29

3 Gossiping Jesus Within and Without Israel: John 1–4   51

4 Gossiping Jesus on the Sabbath and Passover: John 5–6   69

5 Gossiping Jesus at Tabernacles: John 7–11   83

6 Conclusions   103

Bibliography   111

Acknowledgments

MY LIFE HAS BEEN blessed by a number of remarkable friends and mentors. Dr. Mattie Hart of Flagler College is the one who hooked me on New Testament exegesis nearly thirty years ago. She is peculiarly gifted at guiding people to see the Divine, not only in the text, but certainly in her life as well. The peerless biblical studies faculty at Columbia Theological Seminary in the 1990s—Charles B. Cousar, Beverly R. Gaventa, David P. Moessner, Walter Brueggemann, Kathleen M. O'Connor, Stanley P. Saunders, and visiting from Candler School of Theology, Gail R. O'Day—modeled for me a faithful praxis of biblical exegesis that always "hosts the ambiguities" within the Bible, and unabashedly confronts the world with the alternative construal of reality implied within its pages.

I am grateful to my doctoral advisor at the University of South Africa, Pieter F. Craffert, for taking me on as a student soon after the death of my first advisor, H. Richard Lemmer. Pieter deftly guided me in substantially changing the focus of my research from Pauline eschatology to historical Jesus studies. Countless correspondences between us attest to his patience and skill as Pieter fielded many panicked messages while I wandered over the rugged, uneven terrain of securing a viable research question. While I certainly admire his imaginative approach to historical Jesus research, what I most appreciate is Pieter's obvious concern to appropriate his work for the betterment of the life of the people of South Africa. He is, to my mind, a consummate scholar.

My colleagues at Flagler College's Proctor Library have been extraordinary in their support. Thanks to Library Director Michael Gallen, Brian Nesselrode, Blake Pridgen, and Katherine Owens,

Acknowledgments

who patiently waited for me to emerge from the "cave" that is my office where I brooded over this project for a year and a half. Thanks as well to Dr. Timothy J. Johnson, who has consistently offered encouragement in this, and all my academic pursuits over the years.

Special thanks to Ed Bonner for reading the manuscript and offering helpful comments. To my parents, John and Carole, who have always supported my relatively "alternative" avocation as an academic, I offer much love and appreciation. Finally, I am grateful for my wife, Marcia, who has been a constant support and blessing to me for so long—a love letter from God, indeed!

1

Constructing Gossip and Jesus

JESUS THE GENERATIVE FONT

IN THE EIGHTH CHAPTER of Matthew's gospel, the evangelist relates a peculiar story about Jesus and his disciples in a boat, and the rise of a magnificent storm that swamps the boat, all the while Jesus is sleeping. His disciples however, afraid for their lives, plead to their Lord to save them. After waking, then questioning the faith of his disciples, Jesus rebukes the winds and sea so that there follows a great calm. At that point, the narrator describes the disciples' amazement and their questioning, presumably among themselves: "What sort of man is this, that even winds and sea obey him?" (Matt 8:23–27). The disciples' question is not a surprising one, as it emerges in response to an unusual, though not "unnatural," event in Jesus' place and time, and would have certainly generated amazement and talk, in this case, in the form of a question. It is significant that both Mark and Luke include the detail that the question was said "to one another" (Mark 4:41; Luke 8:25), implying that Jesus was not privy to the talk. Indeed, their question, as it appears in Mark, Matthew, and Luke, constitutes what may be described as enscripturated residue of gossip and rumor that would have quite likely accompanied such an event, and thus, residue of

Gossiping Jesus

a particular sort of figure associated with it. The question raised by Jesus' disciples in Matthew's story-world is strikingly similar, if not generative of a similar question raised by a biblical scholar more than two thousand years later:

> Whatever else Jesus may or may not have done, he unquestionably started the process that became Christianity. We have therefore to ask: What sort of man and what sort of career, in the society of first century Palestine, would have occasioned the beliefs, called into being the communities, and given rise to the practices, stories, and sayings that then appeared, of which selected reports and collections have come down to us?[1]

It is remarkable how Morton Smith, a historical Jesus scholar, asks not about the sources first, whether this or that saying or deed of Jesus recorded in the text is authentic or not, but that he wonders about what sort or kind of man would generate the tradition in the first place. This project takes for granted that the traditions comprising the four gospels share something in common, namely, that they are about the same sort or kind of person.

The Gospel According to John has long been recognized to be unique vis-à-vis the Synoptic Gospels for many reasons, including the lengthy discourses uttered by Jesus. This accounts in part for the attention paid to the words of Jesus in John over the centuries. Alternatively, if one is attuned to the talk about Jesus, rather than his words, one may be astonished at the amount of talk about him. The sheer amount of talk about Jesus in John bears witness to the ancient Mediterranean oral culture, while the content and circumstances disclose the intricate relationship between various social processes involved in constituting identity. Although there are a number of texts throughout the Synoptics that can be identified as gossip or rumor about Jesus, John is unique in how such conversation is arranged in the narrative, concentrated in the first twelve chapters comprising Jesus' public ministry, as well as the content and circumstances of the talk. Like the Synoptics, gossip and rumor in John materializes from similar situations, usually because

---

1. Smith, *Jesus the Magician*, 5.

Constructing Gossip and Jesus

of Jesus' words and/or deeds, and in some sort of argumentative discussion with his opponents.

Since the focal point of this book is gossip about Jesus in the Fourth Gospel, the aim is to analyze the role gossip plays, along with other social processes, in constituting him as a social personage.[2] This involves paying close attention not only to gossip, but to other social values and processes that both contextualize and encode such talk in the first-century Mediterranean context. I will thus, proceed by constructing a framework (or "model") for gossip as it actually occurs in the Fourth Gospel narrative. This construction will be done in conversation with modern socio-linguistic research on gossip, modern ethnographies of extant traditional cultures touching on gossip, as well as research already done on gossip and the New Testament.

After constructing a model for gossip, the Fourth Gospel will be read through the framework in order to draw out this peculiar mode of speech actually occurring in the narrative. Once a gossip event is identified, the social situation and generative event can be identified, and the construal of the subject of the gossip may be seen as well. Ancient Mediterranean social values and processes involved will be noted in order to see how gossip colludes with other socio-cultural values and processes to construct Jesus' identity. Subsequently, the process employed here will result in seeing Jesus' social identity in John construed by the complexities of numerous social values and processes, especially gossip, in a way that evinces a plausible historical figure, thoroughly embedded in his time and place.

A Social Scientific Approach

Typically, the historical enterprise attempts to bridge the "historical" or "temporal" gap between the modern interpreter and the

---

2. Such an aim does not exclude rumor, which is often carefully differentiated from gossip. It will become clear that discussion about the latter necessarily involves dealing with the former. Pieter J. J. Botha, "Social Dynamics," has already offered essential treatments of rumor and the Jesus traditions.

individual(s) and event(s) from the past under consideration. A social scientific approach attempts to more precisely to bridge what can be called the "cultural" gap between the modern interpreter and, in the case of this study, the ancient Mediterranean. The challenge lies in understanding social behavior, speech, interactions, expressions, and other coded elements of a different culture—generally referred to as "socio-cultural processes," or "social processes"—and thus, to recognize the various cultural cues that signal meaning-full experiences and events.

Public discourse or talk about a person or subject is common to many different cultures and thus, occurs in different socio-cultural backdrops/contexts with words and/or gestures that are freighted with culturally specific meaning. The challenge to any outside observer is getting to the "domains of reference which derive from and are appropriate to the social world"[3] under observation in order to make sense of such talk. Unless this is done, the resulting interpretation of a gossip event—what generated it, what information is conveyed by it, how it is used by discussants—runs the risk of ethnocentric anachronism.[4] This begs the question: Were people in the Nazareth synagogue complementing Jesus' parents for raising such an eloquent boy when they asked "Is this not Joseph's son?" (Luke 4:22). Or, do such questions about lineage imply something else altogether? Understanding culture, and cultural distance, plays an integral part in making sense of the biblical world that we look in on from the outside. It is a truism, and a peculiar challenge to any outside observer of culturally specific events, that what is understood in any given socio-cultural context, doesn't need to be discussed, and in fact, more often than not, isn't. Thus, it is important to recognize the cultural and social gap between the modern Euro-American context and that of Jesus' first-century Palestine if a reader is going to begin to understand what is actually going on in a story described by one of the Evangelists in a gospel.

    3. Ethnocentrism entails thinking that one's own cultural experience is the same as every other individual's experience throughout the world and through time. In other words, one's cultural experience constitutes "human nature." See Malina, *Christian Origins*, 4.

    4. Malina, *New Testament World*, 10–12.

Constructing Gossip and Jesus

Trying to make sense of a vastly different culture involves conscientiously taking an outsider's perspective on events perceived, described, narrated, experienced, and understood by insiders. In other words, the outsider struggles to recognize the gap, and make sense of events and phenomena in such a way that maintains the cultural integrity of the "the native's point of view" that experiences and describes various phenomena of his/her world differently than an outsider to that world would. To do this is to construct what some social-scientists call a derived etic[5] (or "outsider's") perspective that takes into account the differences between cultures. Thinking about understanding the biblical world, Bruce Malina refers to the neglect of the gap as "inconsiderate reading," and maintains that "without some attempt to reconstruct and enter the social world of the biblical authors, it would seem that one can only be an inconsiderate reader, ethnocentrically anachronistic in highly sophisticated ways."[6]

The process employed throughout this project is straightforwardly social scientific. Since this is the case, a number of processes, presuppositions, and problems will be described in order to show the important advantages of utilizing a social scientific approach (sometimes referred to as "payoff") as well as some of the potential pitfalls. Of course, a key variable in maintaining integrity throughout the research process is self-critical reflection on both process and result. Fortunately, this is one of the characteristic aspects of the social scientific endeavor. Thus, the aim here, is to clearly illustrate the implied backdrop behind the social scientific approach utilized in this project.

Texts from an Orally Other World

A growing number of biblical scholars recognize that the ancient Mediterranean was primarily an oral world. This understanding has been hard to welcome in post-Gutenberg modernity where what is written or in print—the signature/autograph—bears the standard

---

5. Elliott, *What Is Social-Scientific Criticism*, 37–40.
6. Malina, *Christian Origins*, 4.

for authenticity and integrity. For biblical scholarship, what this translates into is a fundamental misunderstanding of the character of texts in an oral world such as that of the Bible. As Werner Kelber has put it, "There is a palpable discrepancy between the dominantly print medium of modern scholarship and the oral-scribal communications world of its subject matter, with the former encroaching upon the latter."[7] Recently, this aspect of the gospel traditions has raised important questions about a number of apparently foundational standards in fields such as form criticism, source criticism (the Two Source hypothesis and "Q"), and the traditioning process that led ultimately to the formation of the canon.[8] The challenge came in recognizing that the way modern Euro-American scholars think of the traditions in terms of textual and inter-textual relationships between writings is not the way traditions in antiquity were perceived. Quite the contrary, in antiquity, even Jesus' antiquity, the oral utterance was held in higher esteem than the written word.[9]

Since in antiquity, where sound was the basic primary channel for communication, the "boundary between written and spoken words" was "porous," and so, the written word was "perceived as having voice . . . vocalized in the act of reading,"[10] it was reasonable for scholars to begin looking at the oral performance of traditions.[11] Public, oral performance was a constitutive part of oral cultures in antiquity and thus, characteristic of early Christianity to the point of it being the primary means for communicating information.[12] Moreover, in the collectivist culture of first-century Palestine, communication was a relational process, accomplished primarily orally, so that "everything that one learns and passes on is done in the

---

7. Kelber, "Orality and Biblical Studies," 25.

8. See Dunn, *Altering the Default Setting*. See also Kelber, "Oral Tradition in Bible and New Testament Studies."

9. See Alexander, "Living Voice"; Ong, *Presence of the Word*; Kelber, "Modalities of Communication"; *Oral and Written Gospel*; Draper, *Orality, Literacy, and Collonialism*.

10. Hearon, "Interplay," 58.

11. See Rhoads, "Performance Criticism 1"; "Performance Criticism 2."

12. See Dunn, "Altering the Default Setting"; Rhoads, "Performance Criticism 1," 9.

context of conversation in a situation."¹³ This underscores the social character of the traditioning processes and is thus crucial to recognizing the background of orality for understanding the vital role gossip played in not only re-collecting the words and deeds of Jesus, but constituting his social identity.¹⁴ Indeed, it is the understanding of this author that gossip (and rumor) reflects the primordial stage of the traditioning process, and that as a peculiarly oral social process—certainly informal, but socially controlled¹⁵—may be understood as a performance insofar as it colluded with other social processes in making sense of a subject.

Living with Models

The process of reading presents its own challenges to a modern reader's understanding of events in antiquity. An outside observer fills in gaps of meaning with subjective knowledge from experiences within his/her own worldview while viewing the behavior of a native "other."¹⁶ The difficulty lies in the fact that authors do not supply details of the social conventions that are background to events described since the intended, ancient audience no doubt would have shared the same worldview. Thus, when a modern outsider reads the ancient text, s/he naturally does so utilizing socio-cultural givens from her/his own world. This underscores the importance of grasping the peculiar complexities of the ancient world's social, cultural, and even cosmological matrices if understanding and responsible appropriation are to be made. This constitutes the practice of "considerate reading" and thus, reasoning behind the careful unpacking of the social world of Jesus' day and place in the chapters below.

13. Rhoads, "Performance Criticism 1," 4.
14. Botha, "Social Dynamics," and "Paul and Gossip"; Rohrbaugh, *New Testament*.
15. See Bailey, "Informal Controlled Oral Tradition."
16. Following Malina, Eric Stewart refers to what I am calling the "subjective knowledge from experiences" as "common sense elements" understood by individuals who share a common worldview. *Gathered Around Jesus*, 31.

Human beings are enculturated beings, that is, they are embedded in cultural systems that to a significant extent, script behavior. It is the socio-cultural script that informs an individual how to act and/or what to do in any given situation and in the presence of others, either in public or in private. Social scientists observe groups of people and the emergence of behavioral patterns, noting the social circumstances, and thus, draw out rather abstract frameworks called models. Bruce Malina defines social-scientific models as "abstract, simplified representations of more complex real world objects and interactions" the purpose of which is to "enable and facilitate understanding."[17] In other words, models describe not reality, but patterns of behavior that emerge given a socio-cultural script.

As tools for studying ancient cultures and texts, models function heuristically, to see material and/or behavior differently. Since models are not descriptions of ontological reality, they should not be elevated to the level of "social law" as if a model could ever prescribe how an individual will behave in every circumstance in every instance, time, and place without any breaks in the pattern. As Philip Esler aptly put it, since models are only heuristic tools, "they are either useful or not, and it is meaningless to ask whether they are 'true' or 'false.'"[18] Nevertheless, the use of models has been critiqued to the extent that an ongoing debate has ensued over their use.[19] On the one hand, a model may be an outsider imposition that, from the start, stacks the deck for a particular construal of events. In this case, a model is seen as forcing the complexities of human behavior into too simple a construct. On the other hand, since human beings already see information in particular ways given a particular social-cultural background—and thus already utilize models—it seems

---

17. Malina, *New Testament*, 17.
18. Esler, *Modeling Early Christianity*, 4.
19. I am aware of, and thus this project presumes, the ongoing debate over the value and use of models for understanding the Bible. Although aware of the possible drawbacks of models pointed out by a number of scholars, the mitigating aspect that undergirds the use of models here is that of self-critical/self-aware usage of such tools. For the discussion, see Esler, *Models in New Testament*; cf. Horrell, *Models and Methods*; and Garrett, "Sociology."

appropriate to *conscientiously* and *self-critically* utilize models since they are useful tools for avoiding ethnocentrism and anachronism. Moving from a model to an ancient text is a process analogous to putting on a pair of glasses tailored specifically to see particular elements of the text that are always there, but not necessarily obvious without the new lenses. In this way, the model functions as a device teasing meaning out of the text with the questions implied in the framework. This process is not a static procedure as the data highlighted in the text through the lens of a model can in turn, compel adjustments to the framework so that a clearer image might emerge. This back-and-forth movement from text, to framework, to text again is a process called "abduction" that serves to mitigate some of the potential pitfalls of the use of models. Bruce Malina describes abduction as a scientific method consisting of three steps: "(1) postulate a model (or theory or paradigm); (2) test the model against the real world experience it relates to; (3) modify the model in terms of the outcome of the test to reduce the misfit by detecting errors of omission or commission."[20]

The construction of a model need not be a process of reinventing the wheel, since gossip is already employed in a number of commentaries on the gospels, even helpfully designated a "reading scenario."[21] The key difference between such models and the one constructed here is the former focuses principally on gossip as observed and commented on in antiquity, while the latter attempts to observe gossip "in action" in the narrative of John's gospel. As will become clear later on, ancient comment on gossip, within and without the Bible, was quite negative. Interestingly, although gossip is considered almost universally to be a vice, often carrying with it devastating social consequences, it was a common phenomenon in the ancient world as attested by the astonishing amount of gossip occurring in the gospel narratives, and especially the Fourth Gospel.

20. Malina, *New Testament*, 17.
21. See Neyrey, *Gospel of John*; Malina and Rohrbaugh, *Gospel of John*; Malina and Rohrbaugh, *Social-Science Commentary on the Synoptic Gospels*.

Gossiping Jesus

Understanding Gossip in Its Cultural Context

With the exception of the last two decades, gossip and rumor research progressed in fits and starts. Nevertheless, there have been valuable sociolinguistic studies of the phenomenon, as well as ethnographies of existing Mediterranean traditional cultures that provide helpful contextual information about the phenomenon, and its social function. Eventually, New Testament scholars would catch on to the promise of such studies, appreciating the significance of gossip research for looking at the gospels in a new way. Although the extent of information gathered about the function of gossip in numerous ethnographies is considerable, I will concentrate on that which is most relevant for the construction of a framework to take to John's gospel.

Gossip in the Mediterranean Context

The most relevant ethnographies of Mediterranean cultures bear out at least four aspects of gossip worth noting. First, gossip emerges out of collectivist societies, that is, non-individualistic cultures where one's identity is embedded in her/his primary group. Thus the phenomenon facilitates maintenance of group boundaries, identity, and relationships.[22] Second, gossip functions to uphold community morals and values, in other words, "shepherding conformity," and maintaining the status quo.[23] Third, gossip is involved in acquiring or ascribing reputation and status in "agonistic," that is, competitive cultures marked by an entrenched concern for the pivotal value of honor, and this in a world comprised of limited good.[24] As such, gossip may take on the character of information control as one attempts to enhance his/her public reputation by initiating the process of construing an event or another individual

22. Gluckman, "Gossip and Scandal," 308–9, 311; Foster, "Research on Gossip," 85; Malina, *New Testament*, 51–70; See also Milgram and Toch, "Collective Behavior."

23. Foster, "Research on Gossip," 86; Gluckman, "Gossip and Scandal," 308.

24. Du Boulay, *Portrait*, 201–2; cf. Gilmore, *Aggression*, 55; Malina, *New Testament*, 25–50, 71–93; Foster, "Interpersonal Relations"; "Peasant Society."

Constructing Gossip and Jesus

or group.[25] Consequently, gossip is recognized as a fundamental social process related to either the transaction of honor/shame, or the reporting of such transactions in a world where honor is conceived to be not only in limited supply, but in fact, already distributed to its limit.[26] Fourth, given that social and consensus reality is constituted by talk, gossip plays an important role in constructing reality, knowledge, and identity as it conveys "shared meanings" through the transformation of generative events into stories that populate corporate memory of communities.[27]

Ancient Evaluation of Gossip

Gossip in antiquity was by and large considered a dangerous vice, and this is easy to illustrate with a few selected texts. All of the following examples have been recognized elsewhere by other biblical scholars.[28]

Plutarch offered much comment on gossip, the following two characterizing it as particularly devious behavior:

> Just as cooks pray for a good crop of young animals and fishermen for a good haul of fish, in the same way busybodies pray for a good crop of calamities, a good haul of difficulties, or novelties and changes, that they, like cooks and fishermen, may always have something to fish out or butcher. (*Moralia* 6.519B)

---

25. Paine, "What Is Gossip."

26. Gleason, "Visiting and News," 501, 503, 516; Lewis, *News and Society*, 13; Gilmore, *Aggression*, 54–55.

27. Gleason, "Visiting and News," 502; Merry, "Rethinking Gossip," 278; Brison, *Just Talk*, 14.

28. For a representative review of the negative attitude toward gossip in antiquity, see Rohrbaugh, *New Testament*, 125–46. See also Malina and Rohrbaugh, *Social-Science Commentary on the Synoptic Gospels*, 366–67. Kartzow offers a more extensive review in *Gossip and Gender*, 41–116. Books and articles reflecting the negative attitude toward gossip in modernity are plentiful. See Meng, "Gossip: Killing Us Softly." See also Sedler, *Stop the Runaway Conversation*.

Gossiping Jesus

> [Gossips] spend their time digging into other men's trifling correspondence, gluing their ears to their neighbors' walls, whispering with slaves and women of the streets, and often incurring danger, and always infamy. (*Moralia* 6.519F)

The following comment, again by Plutarch, situates gossip clearly within the context of an honor-shame culture, especially with its recognition of envy:

> Since, then, it is the searching out of troubles that the busybody desires, he is possessed by the affliction called "malignancy," brother to envy and spite. For envy is pain at another's good, while malignancy is joy at another's evil. (*Moralia* 6.518C)

Lucian is descriptive of the perceived terrible consequences of gossip:

> What I have in mind more than anything else is the slanderous lying about acquaintances and friends, through which families have been rooted out, cities have utterly perished, fathers have been driven mad against their children, brothers against own [sic] brothers, children against their parents and lovers against those they love. Many a friendship, too, has been parted and many an oath broken through belief in slander. (*Calumnia* 1)

Plutarch and Lucian exemplify the nearly universally negative attitude about gossip in Greco-Roman literature where such speech is considered deviant.

In the Israelite world, apart from biblical examples, one sees even more notorious comment on gossip from the Babylonian Talmud and the Mishnah:

> One who bears evil tales almost denies the foundation [of faith]. (*b. Arak.* 15b)

> Any one who bears evil tales will be visited by the plague of leprosy. (*b. Arak.* 15b)

> Of him who slanders, the Holy One, blessed be He, says: He and I cannot live together in the world. As it is said: Whoso slandereth his neighbor in secret, him will I destroy. (*b. Arak.* 15b)

Constructing Gossip and Jesus

> Whoever relates slander, and whoever accepts slander, and whoever gives false testimony against his neighbour, deserve [sic] to be cast to dogs, for it is said, *ye shall be cast to the dogs*, which is followed by, *Thou shalt not take up a false report*, which may be read tashshi. (*b. Pesah.* 118a)

Not only is the pernicious character of gossip maintained throughout, what is noticeable is how many comments on gossip sound like curses, or even threats to those who engage in its practice.

The Hebrew Scriptures are replete with wisdom, comment, and command with respect to gossip:

> You shall not go around as a slanderer among your people, and you shall not profit by the blood of your neighbor: I am the Lord. (Lev 19:16)

> The wise of heart will heed commandments, but the babbling fool will come to ruin. (Prov 10:8)

> One who secretly slanders a neighbor I will destroy. (Ps 101:5)

> You give your mouth free reign for evil, and your tongue frames deceit. You sit and speak against your kin; you slander your own mother's child. (Ps 50:19–20)

> But at my stumbling they gather in glee, they gathered together against me; ruffians whom I did not know tore at me without ceasing; they impiously mocked more and more, gnashing at me with their teeth. (Ps 35:15–16)

The following text remarks on Israel's gossiping about the character of the Lord during their wilderness wandering:

> But you [Israel] were unwilling to go up. You rebelled against the command of the Lord your God; you grumbled in your tents and said, "It is because the Lord hates us that he has brought us out of the land of Egypt, to hand us over to the Amorites to destroy us." (Deut 1:26–27)

This text from Jeremiah reflects how gossip may be part-and-parcel of even in-group dynamics:

> For I hear many whispering: "Terror is all around! Denounce him! Let us denounce him!" All my close friends are watching for me to stumble. (Jer 20:10)

Israelite literature then, confirms gossip's bad reputation even while illustrating its embeddedness in Israelite culture. It is not only among outsiders that one may be gossiped about. Not even the Divine escapes such talk.

The New Testament offers comment on gossip as well, characterizing the phenomenon in much the same way. The following text underscores the relationship between privacy and gossip, illustrating that although the gospel is easily conferred in private space, it is to be proclaimed in public:

> What I say to you in the dark, tell in the light; and what you hear whispered, proclaim from the housetops. Do not fear those who kill the body but cannot kill the soul. (Matt 10:27–28a)

The following three texts reflect the "gossip network" prominent in the ancient oral cultures and important for spreading news as well as constructing public identity:

> But they [two men cured of blindness] went away and spread the news about him throughout the district. (Matt 9:31)

> At once his [Jesus'] fame began to spread throughout the surrounding region of Galilee. (Mark 1:28)

> Jesus went on with the disciples to the villages of Caesarea Philippi; and on the way he asked his disciples, "Who do people say that I am?" (Mark 8:27)

This last text (Mark 8:27), and its parallels, offers an important clue as to how public perception in the first-century Mediterranean partly constructed one's "public self" ("Who do people say that I am?"), and how that identity relates to one's in-group identity, or "in-group self."[29]

Paul was concerned about gossip in his fledgling communities. For example, the church in Corinth when he compares himself and his companions with the Corinthians who consider themselves over-achieving at the kingdom of God:

> When reviled we bless, when persecuted, we endure; when slandered, we speak kindly. (1 Cor 4:12b–13a)

29. "But who do you [disciples] say that I am?" (Mark 8:29). See Rohrbaugh, *New Testament*, 61–76.

Indeed, Botha has demonstrated the importance of the gossip network for informing the Apostle of news (troubles) of his churches.[30] Finally, we look to the Pastoral Epistles for much on gossip as the concern for the household was important for these third-generation Christians:

> Besides that, they [young widows] learn to be idle, gadding about from house to house; and they are not merely idle, but also gossips and busybodies, saying what they should not say. (1 Tim 5:13)

> Avoid the profane chatter and contradictions of what is falsely called knowledge. (1 Tim 6:20b)

> Avoid profane chatter, for it will lead people into more and more impiety. (1 Tim 2:16)

Reading within the framework of a hermeneutic of suspicion, Kartzow has astutely drawn out how the author of 1 Timothy "downloads" the first-century Mediterranean caricature of women's speech, that is, women as "gossips," in order to label young widows in the community as somehow deviant.[31] Kartzow thus illustrates how the phenomenon of gossip was attached to women.[32]

In sum then, although the ancients were relatively ambivalent toward gossip, the practice is basically disparaged in the literature. This is clear throughout the bulk of the literature and stands in interesting contrast to how sociologists and biblical interpreters see vital functionality in gossip of the first-century Mediterranean culture.

---

30. Botha, "Paul and Gossip."
31. Kartzow, "Female Gossipers."
32. That gossip was a stereotypical element of the social construction of women in the ancient world is well known and sheds light on the Fourth Evangelist's attitude toward gossip as such. See also Rysman, "How the 'Gossip' Became a Woman."

Current Studies of Gossip and the New Testament

Pieter J. J. Botha

Probably the most important initial probe into issues related to gossip and rumor as these are explicitly associated with the New Testament, is an article by Pieter J. J. Botha that appeared nearly twenty years ago in *Neotestamentica*.[33] In this study, Botha convincingly advocates the importance of folklore and rumor research for understanding the social processes involved in the transmission of early Jesus traditions. There are several elements in his work that demand the attention of this study given the complexities of the relationship between gossip and rumor.

Utilizing the work of Rosnow and Fine,[34] Botha posits that rumors spring from "raw, confused facts," that their purpose is "precisely that of explaining these raw facts, *to posit a reality*."[35] Moreover, Botha avers that it is "ambiguous events" from which rumors emerge, and that such talk is the result of "a process of collective discussion entailing both an information-spreading procedure and a process of interpretation and commentary."[36] Since changes in the content and shape of rumor are not, according to Botha, due to the failure of human memory, "but rather to the development and contribution of commentaries made throughout the rumour's process," what warrants attention are the realities of the social processes behind such speech.[37] The element of ambiguity that gives rise to rumor is another aspect of the phenomenon that Botha considers in his assertion that ambiguity "arises when one is confronted with an unexpected event, an unexplained incident or incomplete report," that rumor is "the collective transaction through which humans try to fill the gap created by ambiguity."[38]

---

33. Botha, *Social Dynamics*.
34. Rosnow and Fine, *Rumor and Gossip*.
35. Botha, *Social Dynamics*, 211 (italics in original).
36. Ibid., 212.
37. Ibid.
38. Ibid., 220–21.

Botha's initial investigation is suggestive of at least two things related to gossip. First, that the phenomenon, like rumor, emerges in response to unexpected and/or ambiguous events, is particularly relevant since much if not all gossip about Jesus in John arises in response to Jesus' words or deeds that are perceived to be unexpected or out of character for someone of his social status. It is just such unexpected words and deeds that are referred to as "generative events" in this study. Second, that peculiar modes of discourse participate in the construction of reality points specifically to gossip as the initial stage of the construction process, which will be seen to be the case often in John. Precisely the reality under construction in John is not only what happened, but the social identity of the person behind the event, that is, Jesus.

Richard L. Rohrbaugh

In an article entitled *Gossip in the New Testament*, Richard Rohrbaugh provides not only a useful lexicon of words indicative of gossip, but an insightful, functionalist understanding of the social process within the context of the New Testament.[39] Although the lexicon has been criticized for including so many words that it may render the distinction between gossip and "normal speech" imperceptible, the value of it lies not only in its scope through the Hebrew scriptures and the New Testament, but the heuristic value of identifying particular words that may at least, signal to the reader that a gossip event may be under consideration.[40] While the present volume relies more on the social situation, character and content of public speech to identify a gossip event, Rohrbaugh's lexicon will be used from time-to-time to support such a claim.

Significant too, is Rohrbaugh's perceptive identification of types of New Testament texts related to gossip: (1) texts about the topos; (2) reports about gossip occurring—the gossip network; (3)

---

39. Rohrbaugh's article, first published in 2001, reappears in a slightly updated version six years later: *New Testament in Cross-Cultural Perspective*.
40. Rohrbaugh, *New Testament*, 133–38.

Gossiping Jesus

"texts that are themselves gossip."[41] As will become clear later on, it is the third category of gossip that appears most often in the Fourth Gospel, as well as the Synoptics. Rohrbaugh's cue to pay attention to this aspect of the discourse—texts that are gossip—is an important corrective for treatments of the subject relating gossip to the New Testament, including his own.

A most valuable aspect of Rohrbaugh's work is in seeing the functionalist dynamics involved with gossip in the New Testament.[42] Gossip is here understood clearly within the agonistic context of first-century Palestine wherein honor is a pivotal value, and in such a way that takes seriously the oral culture and native speech practices.[43] Rohrbaugh sees gossip functioning primarily to report the transaction of honor, or shame, as these values emerge from public wrangling in the form of challenge-riposte. In other words, once a person has either gained or lost honor in a public challenge-riposte event, the public transmits the results of the exchange through the gossip network.

In sum, Rohrbaugh's important contribution to the study of gossip and the New Testament aims at understanding gossip as a topic of ancient comment and consideration, and as a vital, functional element in live, mundane social processes in the ancient Mediterranean context. Seeing the phenomenon in relation to honor and shame in the ancient agonistic context marks the genius of his insights. This volume departs from Rohrbaugh insofar as it seeks to consider in detail, the social process in action. Thus, in doing so, it builds on Rohrbaugh's work as it seeks to construe gossip as a single thread within the complex fabric that was the constitution of social personages in the ancient Mediterranean.

---

41. Ibid., 145. Van Eck, "Invitations and Excuses," has identified texts that reflect the results of gossip in terms of certain social dynamics.
42. Ibid., 138–44.
43. Ibid., 142.

Marianne B. Kartzow

The most thoroughgoing research relating gossip and the New Testament to date is that of Marianne Kartzow, whose volume *Gossip and Gender: Othering of Speech in the Pastoral Epistles,* offers a deep and detailed treatment of the phenomenon. A detailed review of her book is neither possible nor necessary for the present undertaking. Thus, I will focus on the main thrust of Kartzow's work and those elements of her project most relevant to this project.

In quite convincing fashion, Kartzow demonstrates how the Pastoral Paul of 1 and 2 Timothy and Titus utilizes the culturally embedded, and quite negative impression of gossip as "feminine speech" as a means of othering opponents. In other words by characterizing his opponent's speech as feminine, the Pastoral Paul intends to marginalize and silence their opinions. Indeed, this is his goal with respect to women in the community of believers as well.[44] Of course, the irony here is that because the Pastoral Epistles were intended to be read aloud, and since reading was seen in antiquity as a "re-oralization of written words,"[45] the Pastoral Paul's commentary on gossip, and certainly the talk about his opponents throughout the Pauline corpus, can itself be seen as gossip.

In any event, since the importance of "reinscribing domestic female roles" was a concern of an emerging, non-eschatological church, the "rhetoric of othering" involving the negative female gendering of certain kinds of speech, is disclosed by Kartzow as a particularly effective practice of a patriarchal early Christianity.[46] Her contribution to New Testament scholarship linking ancient speech practices with New Testament texts, and seeing these through a feminist lens, is markedly significant, indeed.

The foundation Kartzow lays on which to build her argument is valuable as it offers a thorough survey of ancient Greco-Roman commentary on gossip, wherein gossip was portrayed as a dangerous vice, and is of course, gendered negatively (female!).[47] It is against this backdrop that she incisively reads the Pastoral Paul.

44. Kartzow, *Gossip and Gender,* 203–4.
45. See Hearon, *Interplay.*
46. Kartzow, *Gossip and Gender,* 204.
47. Ibid., 67–116.

Gossiping Jesus

An especially useful aspect of Kartzow's study is how gossip is defined, or rather, not precisely defined. Instead of offering a static definition of gossip, Kartzow constructs criteria that characterize such speech. The criteria include words within a semantic field for gossip, the content of what is said, the function and effect of the discourse, and the description of the talkers.[48] By not positing a precise definition, Kartzow underscores the transient, pliable nature of gossip that eludes definitive description.

The criteria regarding the content of gossip, and its function/effect are most helpful here. Kartzow draws on modern gossip research to identify the discourse, and thus characterizes it as involving such characteristics as "evaluative talk about third parties who are known but not present," "information about third parties, whether true or false," "intimate details about someone," "a touch of secrecy," "news and scandals," and "rumours heard from 'someone' (anonymous)."[49] The function of gossip as a vigorous and efficient mode of communication, sometimes carrying with it socially dangerous and damaging potential is highlighted as well.[50] Like Rohrbaugh, Kartzow describes a semantic field for gossip as a useful tool for identifying commentary on the phenomenon as well as underscoring common, usually negative, descriptors of the speech.[51]

The importance of Kartzow's research is obvious and has already been underlined above. While Kartzow focuses on ancient comment on gossip, and thus, descriptions of gossip from the perspective of ancient commentary on the peculiar mode of speech, the present work offers a consideration of narrative descriptions of gossip "in action." Gossip "in action" is precisely what this book intends to observe.[52]

48. Ibid., 44–46.
49. Ibid., 45.
50. Ibid.
51. Ibid., 50–65.
52. Since the beginning of the publication process for this project, a number of good works have appeared examining gossip "in action," and its implications. See especially Daniels' "Gossip in the New Testament"; see also Van Eck, "Invitations and Excuses."

Constructing Gossip and Jesus

GOSSIPING A HISTORICAL SHAMANIC FIGURE

The current historical-critical paradigm of Jesus research inclines toward seeing Jesus in John's story-world as someone or something different than the historical figure. This "reigning paradigm" is often described as a process of removing layer after layer of a Tel, and eventually unearthing the authentic nuggets underneath. Alternatively, this project intends to look for the historical figure within John's portrait of Jesus by focusing on a specific social process in concert with others as these are described in the narrative. The implication is that such plausible descriptions of culturally specific social phenomena reflect the initial stages of the traditioning process, and thus, the Jesus tradition. In my attempt to traverse the thorny terrain between story-world and historical figure, I will appropriate the recent work of Pieter F. Craffert in his book *Life of a Galilean Shaman* by relating the situation and content of the gossip in John to the cross-cultural social figure of a shaman as construed within the Shamanic Complex.[53]

Although Craffert's work has received mixed reviews, its significance as a contribution to the historical Jesus conversation is considerable. Not only does Craffert call to question the presuppositions and processes of what he calls "the reigning paradigm," he offers a viable alternative pathway for assessing the gospels toward constructing a historical portrait of Jesus that both accounts for most of the gospel material, and is culturally plausible. Clearly, a valid criticism of the consensus procedures for doing historical Jesus research over the past thirty years is the emphasis on historical-critical, ideational, and literary aspects of the gospels.[54] Craffert's book tenders a useful corrective.

The methodology employed by Craffert is called "cultural bundubashing" and is operative within the framework of anthropological historiography.[55] Without any pretense of certitude, the aim is to ascertain the strangeness of the ancient world, and "how things were" in and around the life of Jesus. In other words, cul-

---

53. Craffert, *Life*, 2008.
54. Elliott, *What Is Social-Scientific*, 13.
55. "Bundubashing" is an Afrikaans referent to "off-road" driving.

Gossiping Jesus

tural bundubashing seeks to account for the historical Jesus while taking seriously the strangeness and pastness of the cultural system implied in the gospels in order to "grasp the meaning, significance, and context of events, phenomena, and people involved."[56] Similarly, the present project adopts the framework of anthropological historiography as it is suggestive of "how things were" around the historical Jesus, and thus, how the historical Jesus was experienced, insofar as this is expressed in descriptions of gossip.

Gossip and the Shamanic Complex

The shamanic complex that Craffert constructs constitutes a matrix of a number of interrelated features and functions of the social type. A shaman is a "religious entrepreneur" who possesses, or is associated with diverse features such as Alternate States of Consciousness (ASC) experiences, spirit possession, and heavenly "sky" journeys. Additionally, a shaman performs various social functions on behalf of a community like healing, divination, control of animals and spirits, ritual, prophecy, and teaching.[57] This "complex" of features and functions provides a "homomorphic model," that is, one that is adaptable to a number of cultural and historical settings while maintaining a general pattern.[58] The various features and functions of the shamanic complex emerge in different combinations from one cultural system to the next.[59] Used as a lens to view the Johannine Jesus, the shamanic complex sketches out all of the

---

56. Craffert, *Life*, 78.

57. Ibid., 135; For spirit possession, see DeMaris, "Baptism of Jesus," and Strecker, "Jesus and the Demoniacs." For ASCs and heavenly journeys, see Craffert, "Altered States of Consciousness," and Pilch, "Altered States." On healing, see Pilch, *Healing in the New Testament*.

58. A shamanic figure in the first-century Mediterranean world will share a number of the same features and functions of a shamanic figure in a twenty-first-century, traditional African culture, though not all of them. In other words, the definition of a shaman is, as Craffert avers, "remade in different historical and cultural settings but with the maintenance of the general pattern." *Life*, 167.

59. Ibid., 167.

various features and functions, thus reasonably portraying Jesus as a shaman.

When a gossip event is identified in John's gospel, and the reader is attuned to the content and character of the speech in relation to the shamanic complex, the connections between the subject of the talk and the shamanic features and functions that materialize are compelling. Moreover, when gossip is observed colluding with numerous other social processes, the complexities comprising the construction of identity can be realized.

In sum, recalling the elements of the methodology of abduction, the shamanic complex provides the stable element in the process of moving back and forth between text and model to see how gossip is operative in constructing identity. Although other social types could be applied similarly to yield different results, it is presumed here that the shamanic complex offers the most plausible social personage.

Constructing a Framework for Gossip

Constructing a viable framework for gossip necessitates engaging the social process at a number of levels including things extrinsic and intrinsic to it. It is important, as well, to distinguish gossip from "general discussion," or "plain talk," since a third party can be the topic of conversation without it involving gossip. Thus, the challenge is to construct a model both precise enough to draw the peculiar discourse out of the narrative, and versatile enough not to exclude texts that may embody gossip. It is to my mind, better to err on the side of pulling in too much talk rather than too little. Moreover, given the character of the method of abduction, what constitutes a gossip event will inevitably be reworked as informed by the text one way or the other.

Extrinsic Features

The features of a gossip event involve elements intrinsic and extrinsic to the actual communicative process. The extrinsic element to gossip is what will be referred to here as a *generative event*. Such events happen within particular social and cultural contexts that carry their own embedded and encoded notions of status quo in terms of behavior and speech. In other words, how people interact with each other is scripted socially and culturally and the script is understood by all. When someone either says or does something outside the margins of the social script, gossip often emerges as a social process of sense making and reality construction. In other words, generative events—unscripted words and deeds—are the catalyst for social discourse that both socially constructs the very event it reacts to, and thus, makes sense of the event vis-à-vis the socio-cultural worldview. It will become clear later on that in the Fourth Gospel's narrative, generative events are often accompanied by other social dynamics and processes involving honor-shame, labeling, stereotyping, and thus, are related to identity.

Intrinsic Features

The intrinsic elements of gossip include those aspects more directly involved in the communicative process. To begin with, gossip involves (1) a number of persons or groups, (2) an oral exchange of evaluative information—either positive or negative—about (3) an absent third party unaware, or even aware, of the talk. Consequently, two individuals may be involved in gossip or even two groups in a large communal exchange of information. Gossip may also emerge within the speech of a group amongst themselves.[60] Being a primary mode of information exchange in non-literate cultures interconnected by "morally homogeneous social networks,"[61] the relation between the gossiper(s), listener(s), and subject are intricate, implying at least a basic level of familiarity. Since gossip is "signed communication," or, face to face talk, the participants likely know, or know about each other and share a mutual understanding

---

60. See Du Boulay, *Portrait*, 127; Gilmore, "Aggression," 62; Guss, "Enculturation," 260, 270; Rohrbaugh, *New Testament*, 127.

61. Merry, "Rethinking Gossip," 277.

Constructing Gossip and Jesus

of what sort of event deserves to be gossiped about.[62] Thus, some sort of implied social intimacy or trust is understood between those involved in gossip. This is important to remember given the ancient Mediterranean collectivist culture populated by numerous in-groups competing for honor, truth, and other resources in the agonistic world of limited good. In such a society, gossip often serves to mark off boundaries between groups, maintaining in-group and out-group distinctions. Interestingly, in John's gospel, gossip emerges among representative groups of people, implying a level of intimacy between them.[63]

It is important to clarify the character of information conveyed by gossip since the relation between cultural attitudes and gossip across culture and time do not always match. In other words, since gossip in antiquity was considered a socially deviant and dangerous form of speech, it is ironic it was so vigorously practiced by men and women, much as it is today. In any event, the information exchanged in gossip must be evaluative somehow, either positive or negative, and this may emerge in three distinctive ways. First, evaluative talk may be tricky to identify since such speech may utilize culturally encoded language that is operative with a particular social situation. For example, when people in the synagogue at Nazareth overhear Jesus' words and respond by gossiping right there in his presence (Mark 6:2–3), the evaluative character of the talk—about where his wisdom comes from, and his lineage—is freighted with culturally specific connotation (negative!) that often eludes modern readers. Second, evaluative discourse may involve disagreement among discussants about the subject. In other words, gossip between two individuals that disagrees about the subject's character reflects an active evaluative process. This sort of gossip is referred to here as "adjudicative gossip." Finally, when one party raises questions to a second party about an absent third party, this may amount to evaluative gossip if the question implies a common social or cultural norm that has been transgressed. Thus, when one asks another why his disciples do not keep kosher, and the

---

62. Rohrbaugh, *New Testament*, 127; Yerkovich, *Gossiping*, 192.
63. Cf. "the people" at 6:14; "the Judeans" at 6:41; "the crowds" at 7:12; etc.

normative view expects disciples to keep kosher, the question itself functions to evaluate some behavior negatively.[64]

When the narrative reports a discussion, the subject of which is absent, it is possible that the discourse is gossip. However, since the subject of gossip may actually be present when the talk is occurring,[65] there are degrees of absence, or better, absence to discourse that need be considered. Indeed, a narrative may offer clues describing the manipulation of space in such a way that creates privacy while rendering the subject absent, thus enabling gossip to emerge. For example, if it is reported that two parties turn toward each other, murmur amongst themselves, or even converse about someone using third-person speech, all the while the subject is actually present, such talk is understood here to be gossip since the subject is rendered absent by such social or communicative variations in speech or physical posture.[66] In fact, gossip is sometimes intended to be overheard by the subject in order to cause harm or to evoke a response.[67] This is the case a number of times in John and will be shown to be an important element of the social dynamic challenge-riposte.

The Contours of a Gossip Event

A gossip event emerges in response to a *generative event*, namely, words and deeds that push the margin of the socio-cultural script. It is a face to face communicative event involving at least two persons or groups engaged in transacting evaluative information, either positive or negative, about a third party subject who is either actually absent or somehow rendered absent to the conversation. A reactive event, gossip is understood here as an attempt to (re)assert or (re)construct the reality of both the event itself and the social

---

64. It will be shown that such questions often embody a challenge demanding a response, thus initiating the challenge-riposte process.

65. See Foster, "Research on Gossip," 81–82.

66. Kartzow underscores how narrative often misses things like body positions and eye movements when describing talk. *Gossip and Gender*, 45.

67. See Handelman, "Gossip in Encounters," 213.

personage involved. From this point the project moves toward examining the social world of Jesus in which gossip was a common occurrence in order to see the various social values and processes comprising the social script of the ancient Mediterranean that, along with gossip, constituted social identity.

2

Gossip in Jesus' Social World

SOCIAL VALUES AND PROCESSES OF JESUS' WORLD

AS A MODE OF speech that naturally materializes in social interactions involving human beings, gossip should be seen embedded in, among, and along with numerous other social values and processes. Looking for such talk within the complexities of a specific social system is challenging, especially in ancient texts that merely describe events without any obvious concern for detailing the socio-cultural matrix within which such events occur. In other words, what is understood, doesn't need to be discussed, and indeed, is not. Ideally then, the payoff is a culturally sensitive reading of the text.

Attempts at describing the complexities of the relationship between numerous social phenomena run the risk of portraying things far more simplistic than they are. In the following description of selected values and processes comprising the social matrix of Jesus' world, the various aspects will be presented separately. The reader is cautioned not to imagine these processes operating singularly in real life, but rather, as strands of a complex fabric that was the social world of Jesus. The aim here is to describe some of the fundamental social values and processes that intersect with one another in public interaction while disclosing how gossip operates within the social matrix.

What is ultimately at issue is Jesus' social identity, or personhood, primarily as it emerges in the story-world of John's gospel, and specifically, by means of a peculiar mode of speech as this is described in the Fourth Gospel. Second, then, what the Johannine Jesus' identity implies, if anything, about the social personage who was the cause for the emergence of the traditions, the communities of faith, and the Fourth Gospel itself can be asked. This of course, presumes a particular way of seeing the traditions about Jesus in John as cultural residue of a social personage, and thus, the Fourth Gospel as a configuration of that social personage.[1] In any event, the values and processes considered below will be analyzed in terms of their role in constituting identity in the first-century Mediterranean context. Thus, by linking social values and conventions with notions of personhood in Jesus' day and place, gossip may eventually be seen playing its part in constructing a rounded character plausibly grounded in the first-century Mediterranean world.

Ancient Mediterranean Collectivism

In ancient Mediterranean cultures, as in modern traditional ones, an individual saw him or herself in terms of a group to which s/he belonged. What this means can be made clear by comparison. On the one hand, in the modern Euro-American context a person sees him/herself as a bounded, unique, self-motivated, and distinctive "whole" (individual) set against other "wholes" (individuals) within a specific social matrix.[2] On the other hand, a collectivist believes s/he is embedded in a primary group, and perhaps a number of secondary groups, the goals of which determine not only his/her behavior within the group and in public, but his/her understanding

---

1. I am indebted to Pieter F. Craffert for articulating the connections I am getting at as "cultural residue" and "literary features of oral phenomena." Likewise, I owe both Pieter Craffert and Pieter Botha together for rightly suggesting the gospels and Jesus as configurations of each other "embedded in the same cultural system." See Craffert, *Life*, 92n10, and Botha, "Submission," 2.

2. See Geertz, "From the Native's," 31.

of self as well. In the ancient Mediterranean, the family stood as one's primary "in-group" and was defined by certain aims like "family integrity, solidarity, and keeping the primary in-group in 'good health.'"³ Indeed, kinship was structured sequentially and outwardly from the central family in-group toward one's tribe and one's nation.

The ancient Mediterranean collectivist person was a "dyadic" person, that is, his/her identity was understood in relation to other members of his/her primary group(s), or in terms of other things like place of origin, clan, or even nationality.⁴ Thus, for example, Jesus is not only "Jesus," but "Son of Joseph," or "Jesus of Nazareth" (Matt 26:71; Luke 4:22; Mark 1:24; John 1:45!). Likewise, Mary from Magdala is "Mary Magdalene" (Matt 27:56; Mark 15:40), Simon is "Simon of Cyrene" (Mark 15:21; Luke 23:26), and Paul is an Israelite descendant of Abraham of the tribe of Benjamin (Rom 11:1). Moreover, the various "facets of self"—private self, group self, and public self—were shaped differently in antiquity than they are today.⁵ For the dyadic individual in a collectivist culture, his/her private self-identity is of little importance compared with the group or public self, since in a collectivist society one's group takes precedence over any individual member. Indeed, in the biblical world, any individual's attempt to assert him/herself as unique from the primary group was considered dangerous to the well-being of the group, and thus, the private self was something to be kept secret.⁶

In antiquity, one's group identity (group self) was preeminent and was fashioned by other members of one's group in what some sociologists describe as a "sequence of embeddedness" that implies an individual's "virtual identity" with the group to which s/he belongs.⁷ Thus, one's role, status, duties, and rights within and without one's group were ascribed to the individual by the group and were learned quickly by the individual.⁸ An individual's primary concern

3. Malina, "Collectivism," 22; Triandis, "Etic-Emic Analysis," 368.
4. Rohrbaugh, *New Testament*, 64; Triandis, *Individualism and Collectivism*, 2.
5 Rohrbaugh, *New Testament*, 69; See also Greenwald, "Self."
6. See Pilch, "Secrecy," 151–57; Rohrbaugh, *New Testament*, 70.
7. Malina and Neyrey, *Portraits of Paul*, 158.
8. Neyrey, "Group Orientation," 94.

regarding identity was how s/he was construed by her/his group first, and second by the public. This phenomenon is clearly illustrated by Jesus' concern over who outsiders (the public) think he is in comparison with who his primary in-group (the disciples) think he is (Mark 8:27–30 and parallels).[9]

Since one's group self was preeminent and matched one's public self, when in public, one was expected to both reflect, and to protect the social status of one's group. In other words, since first-century Mediterranean persons were "sons and daughters of certain fathers and mothers whose honor and shame engulf them,"[10] it followed that any construal of an individual in public, was a construal of the group the individual was a member of.[11] Since the primary group—family, extended family, or secondary in-group—provided the principal social, economic, and religious networking for members, this sort of collectivist self-understanding and embeddedness, at the level of virtual identities, was essential for preserving the group's physical, social, and moral integrity.[12]

Put simply, in the biblical world, an individual's self-concept emerged from however s/he was categorized by her/his in-group, and thus fashioned by the group.[13] Typically, this collectivist self-concept, focused as it was on the group, is what the individual carried into the public arena representing the group in public. Once in the public arena, the individual—engulfed by the group's honor and shame—was in a world where resources were considered to be quite scarce. Indeed, Harry Triandis asserts that collectivism as a social phenomenon emerges mostly in agrarian societies, and specifically as a response to perceptions of resource scarcity where competition for resources is common.[14] Thus, members of large groups experiencing such competitive ("agonistic") circumstances understood

---

9. Rohrbaugh, *New Testament*, 72–75.
10. Malina, *Social World*, 52.
11. Triandis, "Etic-Emic Analysis," 368.
12. Malina and Rohrbaugh, *Social-Science Commentary on the Gospel of John*, 88–89.
13. Elser, "Jesus and the Reduction," 186.
14. Triandis, "Etic-Emic Analysis," 368.

themselves to share a common fate that both defined the group and changed depending on the individual perceptions of that fate.[15]

Limited Good

In the ancient Mediterranean context, the idea of "limited good" was the functional backdrop for a world that saw man as subject to, rather than master of the natural world and all it had to offer.[16] The phrase "limited good" is a social-scientific construct that describes how peasants view their world socially, economically, and naturally. Foster explains this view as "one in which all of the desired things in life such as land, wealth, health, friendship and love, manliness and honor, respect and status, power and influence, security and safety, *exist in finite quantity and are always in short supply.*"[17] The collectivism of Jesus' world, with its group-orientation and all the agonistic social dynamics that materialized in it, was the natural response to seeing the world in terms of what amounted to a zero-sum game, that is, one's gain necessarily resulted in another's loss. What precipitated the view described as "limited good" in the ancient Mediterranean, primarily agrarian world, was the perception of one's sphere of existence as a closed system set in a matrix of other closed systems that were variously interrelated—the village with/to the polis with/to empire with/to the cosmos. In such a matrix, the subsistence needs of a village, for example, relied on forging particular socio-economic relations to urban elites, thus, entering into patron-client relationships in order to ensure access to goods and resources.[18]

Interestingly, since limited "goods" are in finite, limited supply, which cannot increase or be increased, any gain of such "goods" on the part of an individual, family, or other in-group, necessarily

---

15. Ibid.
16. Neyrey, "Limited Good," 123.
17. Foster, "Peasant Society," 296; italics in original.
18. See Hanson and Oakman, *Palestine in the Time of Jesus*, 63–129; Malina, *New Testament World*, 71–93; Stewart, "Social Stratification"; Batten, "Brokerage," and "Patron-Client Institution."

came at the expense of some other(s), and thus, ran the risk of generating envy directed at the one(s) who has gained.[19] Thus, the ancient Mediterranean agrarian peasant was careful not to upset the balance, for example, by receiving a gift or compliment without similarly reciprocating the gesture. Indeed, one would even avoid "getting ahead" among his/her peers in order to sidestep becoming the object of various social-control mechanisms.[20] The key to social balance and stability within the community was maintenance of a "dead level," so the individual would normally, and certainly was expected to do what s/he could, not to upset the status quo.[21]

The way of viewing the world described by the idea of limited good was a constitutive feature of antiquity that stands as the backdrop to the New Testament, and certainly to John's gospel. Relating this idea to Jesus' words and deeds sheds instructive light not only on why Jesus says and does the things he does in John's story-world, but also on the reactions of those near him. It will become clear that the reactions of people to Jesus' words and deeds described in the narrative should be seen in light of limited good, and thus, as in many instances, the initiation of social processes—including gossip—that are attempts to (re)construct "the dead level" that has been thrown out of balance by Jesus.

The particular "limited good" most often at stake in the gospels will be made clear in a moment. For now, our focus is on the collectivist character of ancient Palestine, and the dyadic in-groups that populated it, groups that had to imagine, make sense of, and publicly relate with other outsider groups. The in-group's image of itself, its self-identity, was one that took shape over-against outsider groups, and so it will be helpful to review some of the social phenomena that were involved in processing the group identities of outsiders while maintaining the distinctive character of the in-group.

---

19. Foster, "Peasant Society," 297.
20. Foster, "Anatomy of Envy," 175–82.
21. Malina, "Limited Good," 169–71.

Stereotyping and Labeling

First-century Palestinians were peculiarly ethnocentric, perceiving the world with reference to their broad ethnic group first, and then in terms of subsequent in-groups, kin-groups, and fictive kin-groups.[22] Such a viewpoint resulted in a number of distinctive, dynamic ways that a group would construe itself vis-à-vis outsiders. Two particular dynamics were stereotyping and labeling.

The backdrop for making sense of outsiders by stereotyping and labeling was the value of purity.[23] Purity basically drew the lines in-and-around space, time, and human beings so that everything had its place and was in its place.[24] Thus, purity had to do with social arrangements so that people knew who and where they were, how they fit with respect to other individuals and groups, and how they made sense of themselves in the face of it all. In other words, the matrix of an orderly society was vulcanized by socially constructed expectations of boundaries and place, and so provided benchmarks for identifying when something or someone was out of place, "impure," or "unclean."[25] In the context of an in-group, purity could be compromised from within by group members acting outside their ascribed roles, or from without via infiltration by outsiders. In the agonistic context of ancient Palestine, the concern for maintaining in-group cohesion, solidarity, and identity was such a concern for purity and place. When a threat from an outsider was perceived, the threatened group deployed the processes of stereotyping and labeling to assuage the threat and begin to (re)construct the social world in a way that made and/or maintained sense.

This process of sense-making in the agonistic world of antiquity involved the construction of cognitive maps that allowed an individual, and his/her group to know what to expect when encountering an outsider.[26] The aim was to simplify expectations in order to make knowledge of the outsider easily accessible, their

---

22. Malina, *Social World*, 39.
23. Malina and Neyrey, *Calling Jesus Names*, 36.
24. Pilch, "Purity," 170–73.
25. Malina and Neyrey, *Calling Jesus Names*, 36.
26. Malinia and Neyrey, *Portraits of Paul*, 169–70.

35

actions predictable, and the subsequent assessment easy. Likewise, one's response to an outsider in an encounter would also be readily apparent, indeed scripted, based on previous encounters that usually reified prior assessments.

Stereotyping served to simplify matters adequately. Stereotypes came in numerous forms, often ethnic in character, and carrying labels that ascribed either positive or negative features that contributed to constituting the identities of outsiders.[27] Virgil, for example, generalized about "the Greeks" by means of the sweeping comment: "Hear now the treachery of the Greeks and from one learn the wickedness of all."[28] The results of similar generalizations can be seen throughout the New Testament wherein people are divided into "us" and "them," insiders and outsiders, "Judeans and Greeks" (Rom 1:16; 1 Cor 1:24; Gal 3:28; Col 3:11), "circumcised and uncircumcised" (Gal 2:7–8), and the like.

Stereotypes also emerged in terms of geographical origins as well as status, trade, and even group membership: "Nathanael said to him, 'Can anything good come out of Nazareth?'" (John 1:46); "Is not this the carpenter's son? Is not his mother called Mary? And are not his brothers James and Joseph and Simon and Judas? And are not all his sisters with us?" (Matt 13:55–56a). The motivation behind this was a manageable, fixed notion of what to expect from someone that either validated or (re)constituted the identity of outsiders.

Another form of stereotyping concerned social roles that generated certain social expectations.[29] Thus, for example, there were various roles for fathers and mothers in the family/household, for kings and governors in politics, and for high priests and attendants in the cult. Considering the social world in the New Testament, a number of roles are described such as scribes, tax collectors, and teachers, each of which implied a particular social class that inscribed onto the social cognitive map what to expect from particular persons in public settings based on their social location.

27. Ibid., 171.
28. Virgil, *Aen.* 2.65.
29. Malina and Neyrey, *Portraits of Paul*, 173–74.

Thus, within the public sphere, how people related—what they did or said—did not come as a surprise since it was already scripted. When a person's words or deeds deviated from expectations related to lineage, family/group orientation, or social role and status, and thus did come as a surprise, the socio-cultural cognitive map was (re)adjusted in order to make sense of the deviation. Such (re) adjustment may have come in the form of numerous social sanctions or processes such as a public challenge to the behavior, and of course, gossip.

Related to stereotyping is the praxis of labeling. Labeling involves the identification of a person in terms of some trait or behavior by means of some sort of "tag" or "phrase" encoded either positively or negatively.[30] The act of labeling usually transpires in light of some individual doing or saying something out of place, that is, beyond the boundary lines imagined by society, so that the person is seen as "impure." When someone does or says something "out of place," that person requires assessment either positive or negative.[31] Positive labeling—sometimes called "titular honoring" —materializes in light of a positive assessment of an individual's words or deeds that go beyond socially scripted expectations in some advantageous way. Positive labeling results in the reimagining of social boundaries rather than the enforcement of established ones.

Positive labels are abundant in the gospels. Jesus labels Peter "the rock" (Matt 16:10) and his followers my "mother" and "brothers" (Mark 3:34–35). Likewise Jesus is labeled positively as "teacher" (Matt 12:38; John 3:2), a "prophet" (John 4:19), and "Rabbi" (John 1:49). Indeed, John's gospel is quite full of examples of the practice of labeling, as will become apparent later on. In any event, the application of such titles, or "titular honoring," was normally based on things either said or done by the object of the honoring, and could have considerable positive social consequences.

In contrast to positive labels stand negative labels usually related to the idea of deviance, and deviance labeling. The socially

---

30. Malina and Neyrey, *Calling Jesus Names*, 35.
31. Ibid., 36.

37

defined boundaries serve to alert all when someone is out of place. When the subsequent assessment of that person and his/her behavior was negative, the social response assessing the individual served as a social sanction. Thus, a person would be labeled deviant by means of various "tags" or phrases encoded negatively. Like positive labels, deviance labels are prevalent in the Bible. Jesus is labeled by his opponents as "demon-possessed" (John 8:52), a "sinner" (John 9:24), and derogatively as "King of the Jews" (Matt 27:39). Likewise, Jesus participates in the name calling when he labels Peter as "satan" (Matt 16:23) and his various opponents as "false prophets" (Matt 7:15), "brood of vipers" (Matt 12:34), "hypocrites" (Matt 23:13, 23, et al), and "children of the devil" (John 8:44).

When deployed as a social sanction of behavior out of bounds, deviance labeling is closely operative with the values honor and shame. Thus, on the one hand, such labeling often functions as a form of aggression (sanction) exercised publicly in response to apparently deviant behavior. On the other hand, deviance labeling is used as a defense, or rebuff of a public challenge to a person's words or deeds—a "counter challenge" in the social process of challenge-riposte. Indeed, deviance labeling was a serious attack on another in pursuit of honor given the character of such an attack and the potential social consequences to one attacked.[32]

Labeling, like stereotyping, is not an action taken solely for the convenience of clarifying the identity of an individual or group, but is also for (re)constructing and/or maintaining the social matrix defined as it is by certain boundaries and markers aimed at making sense of the world in a way correlated to the holiness expressed by God in God's created order.[33] Indeed, the construction of the world, subjectively experienced from group-to-group, of course, was at stake.

---

32. Ibid., 37.
33. Cf. Neyrey, *Paul in Other Words*, 26–29.

Talking in Stereotypes and Labels

In discussions about others, especially outsiders, people in antiquity were no less likely to employ labels and stereotypes than are Euro-Americans today. While stereotypes and labels usually carried negative connotation, and thus, discourse using them construed a subject negatively too, such discourse served easily to both construct and maintain the cognitive map of the world, and nurture the group self-identity of persons in Jesus' world. To be sure, stereotypes and labels abound in the Fourth Gospel and, as will become clear, were utilized often to (re)construct a subject and/or (re)constitute the status quo shaken by strange, unscripted words or deeds.

JESUS' IN-GROUP: A FACTION

To this point we have considered how collectivist groups—kin-groups and fictive kin-groups—in an agonistic culture of limited good, carved out cognitive maps in order to make sense of their place in the world among other groups, to "place" and make sense of outsiders, and to inscribe expectations of outsiders so that encounters with them were scripted, holding no surprises. Although Jesus' in-group can be described as a fictive kin-group, it is better to see his group as a particular kind of in-group given its origin and character, that is, as a type of coalition called a faction.[34]

A coalition is a group gathered for a limited period of time for specific purposes, loosely connected, informal, and voluntary. Membership in a coalition did not override more permanent loyalties such as those to kin-groups. However, a particular kind of coalition called a *faction* was a group formed around a central, charismatic individual who recruited followers for a specific purpose over a given amount of time. Members of a faction exercised exclusive loyalty to, and shared the vision and goal of the one who called the group into existence. Jesus and his close followers together, formed such a faction. Rivalry between factions was expected

---

34. On coalitions and factions, see Malina, "Early Christian Groups"; See also Malina and Rohrbaugh, *Social-Science Commentary on the Synoptic Gospels*, 342–43.

along with the competition for limited resources such as honor and truth.

Groups that were not rooted in kinship or lineage, materialized in the ancient Mediterranean because of a charismatic individual's recognition of a need for some kind of change, and the impression that conditions for such change were possible. According to the gospels, Jesus' ministry/movement followed that of John the Baptist, and was one with a rather clear goal, that is, to proclaim the coming kingdom of God and to evince this primarily by means of healing (cf. Matt 10:1–11; Luke 9:1–5; Mark 6:7–13).

The Words of Jesus: Anti-Language

Jesus' primary in-group, or "faction," can be referred to as an anti-society. An anti-society is a group established within an overarching, majority society as a conscious alternative to the dominant society.[35] As part of its active resistance to status quo, such a group would often develop its own insider language, or "anti-language," that was constituted by relexicalized words or phrases, and sometimes by a new vocabulary. Relexicalization involved the use of words commonly shared between the anti-society and the outsider society with the word's taking on new meaning for the anti-society. Likewise, objects and/or actions signified by common words would be assigned completely new vocabulary by an anti-society. As Halliday points out, the process was based on the principle of same grammar, different vocabulary.[36] Words relexicalized or invented by an anti-society would often emerge in and around certain activities peculiar to the subculture and that most obviously set it apart from the majority, outsider society.[37]

The construction of anti-languages served strategic purposes for the anti-society, or faction in which it emerged, not the least of which was to help the group realize its *raison d'être* with the help of some secrecy as meanings would escape outsiders and thus,

35. Halliday, "Anti-Languages," 570.
36. Ibid., 571.
37. Ibid.

Gossip in Jesus' Social World

hopefully advance the faction's goal(s). Clearly, anti-language would help reify and nurture group self-identity over-against an outside world hostile to the group. Interestingly, anti-languages—as do languages normally—served to create and maintain an alternative reality for the group employing it.[38] Since language is a reality-reifying force for societies and cultures, the importance of the emergence of anti-language in Jesus' in-group cannot be understated, and indeed, sheds important light on social processes involved in the construction not only of subjective reality, but of social identity as well.

Words Strange and Generative

The language used by Jesus and his disciples in John's gospel is often portrayed as a stumbling block to outsiders who either struggle to understand them, or challenge their legitimacy. Understanding indicates that one is part of, or becoming part of Jesus' in-group, while misunderstanding indicates the opposite, and if persistent, results in vituperative argumentation. The reason the language shared by Jesus and his group was often troubling to outsiders is because of its peculiar characteristics that dynamically set it apart from the language of the majority of outsiders.

By identifying Jesus' group as a faction, biblical scholars have been able to see the often virulent reaction to Jesus' words by his opponents, or even the crowds, in new light. The social dynamics at work were intricate, and easily charged a situation. Words designed to stump outsiders while encouraging insiders, elicited hostile disdain when articulated in public since they destabilized the consensus socio-cultural world in a way that pushed outsiders to reassert the world. In other words, outsider reaction to insider anti-language would often come in the form of some sort of public sanction, usually a challenge that demanded a response. The result of the agonistic interaction, called challenge-riposte, was subsequently recognized and verified publicly, and then reported via the gossip and rumor network. Sometimes, public sanction challenging strange words or deeds would take the form of gossip that, when

38. Ibid., 573–76.

uttered publicly with the intent of being overheard by the subject, operated as a peculiarly effective "public" challenge. Details of this interesting dynamic will be unpacked further below.

Honor and Shame

To this point we have considered a number of social institutions and processes of Jesus' world in order to set a framework through which to see the text of John's gospel. Before moving to specific texts in John reporting gossip, it is important to consider the peculiarly catalytic social value that was operative in Jesus' world, namely honor, and this in concert with it's apparent opposite, shame. Throughout the Fourth Gospel, and indeed the Synoptics too, the pivotal value of honor is inscribed in nearly every interaction—private and especially, public—described in the narrative. In other words, honor is the backdrop and catalyst for nearly every social interaction between Jesus and those described as outsiders or opponents in the gospels. Moreover, nearly every interaction between Jesus and someone outside his faction can be characterized as agonistic since it occurs in a world dominated by the idea of limited good. Honor in Jesus' world was a limited good, so there was only so much to go around. Thus, every interaction potentially resulted in honor gained and honor lost.

A Versatile and Enduring Model

As articulated earlier in chapter 1, a social-scientific model is an abstraction, or representation of the complexities of real world objects and interactions. In other words, a model is a scholarly construct that does not describe reality, but hopefully enables understanding by underscoring patterns of behavior. There is a prevailing and helpfully enduring model of honor-shame that New Testament scholars employing the social sciences to understand biblical texts have been using for nearly the past 35 years. This enduring model was constructed by Bruce Malina and, despite both criticism and useful tweaking, has remained the benchmark for making sense of honor and shame in the Bible.[39]

According to Malina, honor is "the value of a person in his or her own eyes (that is, one's claim to worth) *plus* that person's value in the eyes of his or her social group."[40] In light of the recent work on the honor-shame model by Zeba Crook, Malina's definition of the pivotal value can be fine tuned to more accurately reflect the collectivist culture of the biblical world as well as the social construction of identity. Following Crook then, honor is the value bestowed on a person publicly and by his or her social group. This definition rightly emphasizes that the most important aspect involved with honor is the public recognition of it by the PCR—that is, the "public court of reputation."[41] In other words, honor—bestowed by various means to be illustrated later—must be acknowledged as such by the public consensus, or it is not honor at all. Thus, every emanation of honor, as well as the social processes involved in the transaction of honor and shame, was totally dependent on it being recognized, and then distributed by the public. Such recognition, and the criteria evoking it, was by no means universal throughout the ancient Mediterranean, but was rather, local, and somewhat unpredictable. Indeed, Crook describes the PCR as a rather "fickle arbiter of honorable and shameful behavior."[42]

Commenting on honor in antiquity, Richard Rohrbaugh, working closely with Malina's model, avers honor as "the goal, the passion, the hope of all who aspire to excel . . . dear to life itself."[43] The extent to which the concern over honor permeated the ancient

---

39. Malina, *New Testament World*, 27–57. Malina's model has been utilized most helpfully by Richard Rohrbaugh, "Honor: Core Value in the Biblical World." Zeba Crook, "Honor, Shame, and Social Status Revisited," offers a refreshingly respectful, timely, and valuable "tweaking" of Malina's model. I will attempt to employ Crook's adjustments in the description of honor-shame below.

40. Malina, *New Testament World*, 30; See also Pitt-Rivers, "Honour and Social Status," 21.

41. Crook, "Honor, Shame, and Social Status Revisited," 593.

42. Ibid., 610.

43. Rohrbaugh, "Honor," 109.

Mediterranean is extraordinarily clear in ancient authors. In his *Histories*, Tacitus relates a story of how the emperor Vespasian was approached by both a blind man and a man with a crippled hand, and was asked for healing by both. Vespasian's reply discloses his keen concern for honor:

> At first Vespasian ridiculed and repulsed them. They persisted; and he, though on the one hand feared the scandal of a fruitless attempt, yet, on the other, was induced by entreaties of the men and by the language of his flatterers to hope for success. (*Hist.* 4.81)

Writing of the "great-souled man" in his *Nichomachean Ethics*, Aristotle articulates the primacy of honor:

> Worth is spoken of with reference to external goods; and the greatest external good we should assume to be what we render to the gods, the good most aimed at by people of worth, the prize of the noblest. Such is honour, since it is the greatest external good. (*Eth. Nic.* 3.1123b)

In an oft-quoted text, Xenophon supposes the concern for honor to be something that set human beings apart from animals, but not all humans:

> In this man differs from other animals—I mean in this craving for honor. In meat and drink and sleep and sex all creatures alike seem to take pleasure, but love of honor is rooted in neither the brute beasts nor in every human being. But in them in whom is planted a passion for honor and praise, these are those who differ most from beasts of the field, these are accounted men and not merely human beings. (*Hiero* 7.3)[44]

Standing in striking relief to honor, was shame. Shame was something to be avoided at nearly all costs. In the collectivist ancient

---

44. Quoted in Rohrbaugh, "Honor," 110. Rohrbaugh offers an extensive list of texts from antiquity to illustrate what he claims to be the "universality" of honor as illustrated in ancient authors. That the concern for honor and shame permeated the ancient Mediterranean is by no means a claim that such concern was universal. Recent ethnographic research of two traditional Mediterranean societies suggests honor-shame, and the public recognition of it, were not universally overriding concerns. See Brogger and Gilmore, "Matrifocal Family in Iberia."

Mediterranean world, an individual's publicly recognized shame was borne by his/her family and/or primary in-group. The New Testament describes "weeping and gnashing of teeth" as the typical reaction to being publicly shamed (Matt 8:2; 13:42; Luke 13:28, et al).[45] Having shame, on the other hand, was something positive and encouraged, and typically attributed to women. Having shame is being properly concerned over the careful maintenance of one's honor, and thus, the honor of one's family or in-group. Indeed, having shame was considered a form of wisdom especially embodied in women (Prov 1:25–26; 8:1).[46]

Honor Ascribed and Distributed

There are two types of honor reflected in the gospels—ascribed honor and distributed honor.[47] Honor was publicly ascribed to an individual due to the nobility of his/her family conferred at birth, or by grant of royalty or someone of high social standing, upon someone of lower social standing. Of course, such "ascribed honor" was not honor unless recognized as such by the PCR.

A considerable number of biblical texts illustrate the idea of ascribed honor:

> See, everyone who is fond of proverbs will say of you, "Like mother, like daughter." (Ezek 17:44)
>
> All things have been handed over to me by my Father. No one knows the Son except the Father, and no one knows the

---

45. Rohrbaugh, "Honor," 112.
46. Ibid., 113.
47. Malina's model identifies the two types of honor as "ascribed" and "acquired." In my attempt to implement Crook's adjustments to the model, the use of "distributed" rather than "acquired" is employed and thus, recognizes that the latter better reflects the collectivist culture of antiquity than the former. "Acquiring" honor implies a subjective individual concern, while "distributed" honor underscores the primary role of the PCR in the transaction of honor and shame. I see no reason for substituting "ascribed" with "attributed" since both words practically mean the same thing. Indeed, "ascribed" is preferred since it reflects the social "scripting" involved when the PCR ascribes honor to a person and his/her group.

Father except the Son and anyone to whom the Son wishes to reveal him. (Matt 11:27)

He who spoils his son will have wounds to bandage, and quake inwardly at every outcry. (Sir 30:7)

Ascribed honor is reflected conspicuously by the genealogies found in the Gospels of Matthew and Luke (Luke 3:23–28; Matt 1:1–17) and the prologue of John's gospel (1:1–18). Indeed, genealogies in antiquity reflected ascribed honor the same way portraits or marble busts of previous monarchs served to ascribe a reigning monarch with honor in a sort of cumulative fashion, connecting them to a long line of honorable predecessors. Seneca articulated the potential inherent in ascribed honor:

> So-and-so was the father of great men: whatever he may be, he is worthy of our benefits; he has given us worthy sons. So-and-so is descended from glorious ancestors: whatever he may be, let him find refuge under the shadow of his ancestry. As filthy places become bright from the radiance of the sun, so let the degenerate shine in the light of their forefathers. (*Ep.* III, 4.30.4)[48]

Thus, a person bore the honor of his or her family and the collective honor of the family's ancestry as that honor was borne throughout the family's history.[49]

"Distributed honor" was bestowed on an individual by the PCR in approving recognition of the individual's successful acquisition of honor usually manifested in the form of the social process called challenge-riposte. Challenge-riposte involved two individuals, usually but not always two males of equal status publicly hassling one another in order to gain honor from the other. A challenge between two individuals could come in a positive form via compliments, praise, or gift giving. Conversely, a challenge could come negatively by means of questions, dares, or even outright threats. Once a challenge was made and recognized as such by the one challenged, a response (riposte) would be offered. The exchange could go on however, if an initial challenge was responded to with a

---

48. Cited in Rohrbaugh, "Honor," 118–19.
49. Malina, *New Testament World*, 29.

counter challenge. If the challenge is met successfully, then honor is maintained; if not, it is lost. Of course, the exchange of honor only occurred when/if the PCR recognized that such an exchange of the limited good was warranted.

A good example of challenge-riposte can be seen in Matthew's gospel when Jesus aggressively initiates the process by asking the Pharisees whose son is the Christ (22:41-46). Their response is shown by Jesus to be inadequate, and thus results in their no longer engaging Jesus publicly with questions (22:46). Since nearly every public, social interaction could potentially result in such a competitive exchange, why Jesus' culture is described as "agonistic" to scholars is no surprise.

Sometimes a challenge was made to the social status quo when an individual publicly spoke words, demonstrated knowledge and understanding, or some other gift/skill not normally associated with that individual's status. Because of the common perception of limited good, such "honor claims" were rarely met with approving acceptance, but more often with social sanction in the form of a challenge, or rather, a counter challenge. Again, the scene in the Nazareth synagogue is illustrative (cf. Mark 6:1-6; Matt 13:53-58; Luke 4:16-30). Jesus' sagacious public preaching was perceived as an inappropriate honor claim given his social status (son of an artisan whose parents are known), as if the limited goods of wisdom and graciousness had been somehow stolen by Jesus. Thus, in a manner of speaking, Jesus was seen to be flaunting these newly acquired goods publicly. But because someone of his social status was not supposed to have access to such goods, his audience "took offense" (Mark 6:6).

Gossiping in Jesus' World

The above survey of various social values and processes in place in Jesus' Mediterranean world describes the dynamic backdrop that catalyzed social interaction and discourse, and provided the necessary materials for the construction and maintenance of identity. Knowledge of these diverse social elements can be used to look at the traditions in John's gospel differently, to see speech and talk differently, and in a way that underscores how talk constructs social personages and social reality. Used as a heuristic lens to read the Fourth Gospel's narratives, knowledge of these values and processes make it possible to see how Jesus' identity is construed in John's story-world.

To begin with, first-century Palestine was a collectivist culture where the principle institution was the family, the extended family, or kin-group. It was often the case that a person was also a member of another group, a fictive kin-group, coalition, or faction. An individual's identity was embedded in his/her primary group in a sequence of embeddedness so that one's identity was determined by one's primary group members. In other words, one's identity was not constituted by an individual, bounded self-image, but in good allocentric fashion, by significant others. Because an individual's identity was constructed by the group, in public that individual bore the identity and social status of the group.

People in antiquity were attuned to outsiders ethnocentrically, that is, in contrast to, and in terms of their primary group. People were equipped with stereotypes and labels to make sense of outsiders or others who acted in ways socially unscripted or unexpected. On the one hand, as mentioned earlier, such labels and stereotypes served to prepare persons for encounters with outsiders—what to expect and how to proceed socially. On the other hand, labels and stereotypes were also deployed to make sense of unexpected or unscripted words or behaviors in such social encounters. In Jesus' time and place when persons encountered one another outside of the safety of their primary group and place, such meetings were normally accompanied by a certain level of anxiety.

Mining and Mapping a Social Process

John's gospel is full of long discourses between Jesus and individuals or sometimes groups of individuals. Since there is no lack of talking going on in the Fourth Gospel, there is a considerable amount of material to look at for gossip. The framework for gossip outlined thus far, draws nuance out of many texts that would not normally be seen as involving such speech. Spotting a gossip event involves identifying basic elements of the process—a generative event, discussion between two persons or groups about a third party either actually or rendered absent, and positive or negative evaluation of the subject. These three elements comprise a bare minimum that may at times be nuanced in particularly intricate narratives such as John 6–8 and John 9.

In the entirety of John's gospel, no less than forty-two texts are related somehow to the social process of gossip. While at least thirteen of these texts are either about gossip as such, or report gossip and/or the gossip network, the majority describe the process of gossip "in action." Some observations about the distribution of gossip throughout the Fourth Gospel are in order. First, the texts about gossip (John 2:23–25 and 4:42) appear to tacitly offer negative appraisal of the speech. The former text implies Jesus' reticence to trust himself to people because of the gossip network's reports about his signs, while the latter negatively genders gossip as feminine "chatter." Thus, the texts about gossip only seem to reflect cultural bias toward the social process, rather than offering explicit comment on such talk. Indeed, this adds to the cultural plausibility of the two scenarios. Unlike the Pastoral Epistles explicit negative criticism of gossip, the Fourth Gospel, being a narrative, embeds the process into the story-world of John, just as gossip was embedded in Jesus' social world. Second, since the majority of gossip texts are descriptive reports of gossip "in action," and in response to Jesus' words and deeds, it is likely the Evangelist was aware of the social process as part of the experience of Jesus during his life and after his death and resurrection. This in turn, implies that such cultural stories about Jesus in John are literary residue of the experience of a historical figure. Third, most of the discourse between Jesus and others, especially his opponents, occurs in the first twelve chapters, that is, what some scholars have called the Semeia-Quelle, or the "Signs Source." As it turns out, the bulk of the talk in these chapters can be seen as gossip. It is significant as well, that much of the gossip emerges in antagonistic situations reflecting the agonistic character of public interaction between persons of different groups competing for limited resources. Seen from a form-critical perspective, John's controversy narratives, although bearing some resemblance to many of the "pronouncement-stories" found in the Synoptics, do not resemble the speech conventions of the Synoptics as much as the Fourth Evangelist's own creative use of prior traditions. Nevertheless, the cultural plausibility of the controversy narratives remains high.

The aim of the chapters that follow is to isolate and analyze gossip "in action" in John's gospel in order to understand the role such talk plays in constituting Jesus as a social personage, specifically, a shamanic figure. This project takes for granted that Jesus can be seen as a shamanic figure, so the goal is to draw out how a peculiar mode of speech—understood within the framework of a collectivistic, agonistic honor-shame cultural matrix of the first-century Mediterranean world—is operative along with other social dynamics in constituting Jesus as a social personage.

3

Gossiping Jesus Within and Without Israel

John 1–4

Jesus' First Disciples

THE GOSSIP IN JOHN 1:19–51 is important in constructing Jesus' identity for the readers of the gospel, implied "insiders," and for Jesus' first and closest followers. In a way, the Evangelist narrates the social construction of Jesus' identity by his primary in-group, thus plausibly reflecting the Mediterranean collectivist self, construed as it was dyadically by the group, rather than by the individual. This gossip by Jesus' first followers does not simply appear, but is carefully contextualized as it follows the prologue (1:1–18) that clearly articulates both Jesus' identity (the Word), and his origins (from above, or, the Father). The gossip is further contextualized by the testimony of John the Baptist, and his gossiping about Jesus to some of his own disciples.

Gossiping Jesus

The Baptist's Testimony

The prologue is a theologically loaded beginning to a gospel deeply concerned with Jesus' identity as it makes clear from the first that Jesus is "the Word" who was "with God" and "was God," and this from "the beginning" (1:1-2). The Word, identified as "God the only son" (1:18), and God enjoy an intimate knowledge of, and communion with one another.[1] Significantly for a gospel interested in Jesus' identity, the Word that was in the world was nevertheless, not known by the world (1:10). Thus, the Evangelist invites the reader to both observe the subsequent construction of Jesus by "the world" that does not know him, and to engage in the construction of Jesus along with the other insiders of the narratives—Jesus' disciples, including "the twelve." How the Word got from where God is to the world was by means of incarnation (1:14). That Jesus is the Word "enfleshed" is of considerable import for the Fourth Gospel's notion of his nature, perhaps to underscore that the Word did not only "seem" to be here on earth, but was grounded substantially in this world by flesh.[2] In other words, it is made clear that Jesus "the Word" comes from God, makes God known (*exēgeomai*; 1:18)[3] and thus, has his origins in the heavens.

Priests and Levites suggest to John the Baptist that if he is not the Messiah, then he may be an end-time prophetic figure such as Elijah (cf. Sir 48:10-11) or "the Prophet" (Deut 18:15, 18). It is noteworthy that according to tradition, Elijah was taken up into heaven, remaining alive until his return before "the day of the Lord" (2 Kings 2:11; 2 Chron 21:12; Mal 3:1). Moreover, Enoch imagines Elijah's return even before the appearance of the apocalyptic lamb (1 Enoch 89:52; 90:31)—an arresting prolepsis of the Baptist's

---

1. Barrett, *Gospel According to St. John*, 170.

2. Ernst Käsemann, *Testament of Jesus*, famously described the Christology of the Fourth Gospel as a "naïve Docetism," a description that has not been well received. See also Larsen, "Narrative Docetism," 346-47.

3. In this way, Jesus "interprets" and unveils the character of the Divine to human beings. See Keener, *Gospel of John*, 1:424. Such "making known" of the Divine was common to Hellenistic religions encompassing the idea of "telling at length," or "recounting a narrative" about the Divine. See Moloney, *Gospel of John*, 47; Barrett, *Gospel According to St. John*, 170.

construal of Jesus as "Lamb of God" (John 1:29).[4] "The Prophet" in mind at 1:21 is likely the "prophet like Moses" expected to come and perform various forensic and legislative duties (1 Macc 4:41-50; 14:1; Acts 3:22; see also John 6:14; 7:40). The important point to remember here is that being associated with such "prophetic" figures implies something about such figures journeying from the heavenly realm to the earthly realm, and is thus, a significant element of the identity of anyone seen as such. The Baptist removes any confusion about his own identity, clarifying that he is neither the Messiah, nor Elijah, nor even "the Prophet," thus implying such honorific titles to Jesus (1:20-21).

The Baptist's next construal of Jesus occurs on "the next day" (1:29) when he declares Jesus as "the Lamb of God who takes away the sin of the world," and follows this with a vivid description of an alternate state of consciousness experience (ASC) during which he both witnessed Jesus being possessed by the Spirit, and heard a voice from the heavens (1:32-33).[5] Such an experience on Jesus' part reflects what was common in antiquity surrounding the inauguration of a holy man of God.[6] The Baptist emphatically bears witness to this inauguration by describing his own ASC experience, and suggesting Jesus enjoys God's unique and abiding favor,[7] as well as the important soteriological function of the Lamb, that is, to "take away the sin of the world" (see Isa 53:7).

The lamb came to be associated with the sacrificial cult of ancient Israel since lambs were the primary victims at the Temple

---

4. Brown, *Gospel According to John*, 47.

5. Malina and Rohrbaugh describe ASC experiences as "conditions in which sensations, perceptions, cognition, and emotions are altered. Such states are characterized by changes in sensing, perceiving, thinking, and feeling. When a person is in such a state, the experience modifies the relation of the individual to the self, body, sense of identity, and the environment of time, space, and other people." *Social-Science Commentary on the Synoptic Gospels*, 327-29. See also Pilch, *Altered States*. For the modern, Euro-American, such experiences are normally considered pathological and thus, the knowledge gained from them, illicit. This is of course, an ethnocentric and anachronistic conclusion.

6. Malina and Rohrbaugh, *Gospel of John*, 35-36.

7. Neyrey, *Gospel of John*, 53.

Gossiping Jesus

(Exod 12:11–12; 29:38–42; Lev 16:21; Num 28:11, 16–19, et al). In the New Testament, the lamb is seen similarly in a cultic context, and thus associated with Jesus (e.g., Acts 8:32; 1 Pet 1:19).[8] At John 1:29 and 36 the Baptist combines the two ideas of the paschal lamb (cf. 19:29, 36; Exod 12:22, 46) and Jesus bearing sins (Isa 53:4, 12), and indicating that Jesus was a new sacrifice, superior to the present cultic sacrifice of the Temple and thus, a perfection of Judaism's ordinances and institutions (John 2:19; 4:21; 5:17, 39, 47; 6:4; 10:1; 13:34).[9] Thus, by referring to Jesus as the Lamb of God, the Baptist's gossip about him suggests Jesus' mediating power with the divine world. Such mediating power to put things right between the Divine and the world is a function associated with a shamanic figure, and is here ascribed to Jesus by means of gossip (1:36).[10]

The Baptist's ASC at 1:32–34 is essentially the Fourth Gospel's version of Jesus' baptism, although sharing little in common with the Markan version employed by Matthew and Luke. Interestingly, all versions of Jesus' baptism are similar to the initiation process of a shamanic figure marked by spirit possession, visions, and auditions. Being possessed by the (Holy) Spirit is a cultural interpretation of a bodily possession experience that implied an impersonal force taking possession of, or "filling" a person. Indeed, in Jesus' world, this was viewed as a way of being to the extent that the one possessed somehow became who/whatever s/he was possessed by.[11] Although cross-cultural research shows that ancient societies could view such possessions negatively or positively—positively if the one possessed brings benefits to the community, and negatively if the possession brings "insanity" or is not connected to a ritual[12]—the Baptist's telling of his ASC implies he viewed Jesus' spirit-possession favorably. An important component of the life of a shamanic figure, Jesus' spirit possession described by the Baptist and eventually transmitted in his gossiping about the Lamb of God (see below),

---

8. Jesus is associated with the lamb twenty-eight times in the Apocalypse alone.
9. Barrett, *Gospel According to St. John*, 176–77.
10. Craffert, *Life*, 340–41.
11. Ibid., 214–15, 231–32; see also Matt 12:18; Luke 4:18.
12. DeMaris, "Possession, Good and Bad," 19–20; Craffert, *Life*, 230

thus construed the baptism as a cultural event implying Jesus was experienced as being spirit-possessed throughout his career.

All in all, the Baptist's testimony to Jesus reflects what has already been proffered by the prologue; Jesus is the preexistent Son of God. In other words, Jesus' origins from the Father in heaven, and his identity as the Son of the Father in heaven becomes integral to how Jesus is ultimately constituted in this gospel. Indeed, from the standpoint of characters in John's story-world, the Baptist offers the inaugural testimony to Jesus' identity, origins, and function even while being simultaneously subordinated to Jesus by the Evangelist. In any case, his testimony comes first, and is soon followed by that of several other characters understood as "insiders."

The Disciples' Talk

On "the next day" again (*tē epaurion*, 1:35; see also 1:29, 43), the Baptist gossips with two of his own disciples about Jesus, who walks by, apparently unaware of their talking: "And as he saw Jesus walking by he said, 'Behold, the Lamb of God.' And the two disciples heard him say this, and followed Jesus" (1:36–37). This gossip about Jesus' identity, apparently generated by John's ASC experience (1:32–33), is in the form of titular honoring and implies positive evaluation and construal of Jesus by John that was already conveyed by the Baptist the previous day. John's disciples, although passively involved in the gossip encounter as listeners (*akouō*, 1:37), upon hearing the Baptist's description of Jesus, leave John to follow him. Such a quick exit from one in-group (John's) to another may indicate that the two were only marginal members of John's group.[13] Indeed, such a transfer of allegiance implies the agonistic background of honor-shame given John's vigorous denial of the honorific titles brought to him from those sent by the Judeans at 1:19–28.[14] Later on in the story, the Baptist will forcefully reiterate these denials,

---

13. Malina and Rohrbaugh, *Gospel of John*, 54–55.

14. I will render the Greek "*hoi Ioudaioi*" as "the Judeans" rather than "the Jews" throughout. See Malina and Pilch, *Social-Science Commentary on the Letters of Paul*, 371–74; Pilch, "Are there Jews and Christians in the Bible?"

specifically drawing out his lower social status vis-à-vis Jesus as he explains the necessity of Jesus' increase and his own decrease (3:30; see also 5:36; 10:41).[15] In any event, the gossip reflects a process whereby legitimating titles are applied to Jesus via gossip to potential disciples, thus acknowledging Jesus' honor, all of which is soon followed by Jesus' own revelation(s) of profound significance.

Upon hearing the Baptist's description of Jesus as Lamb of God, the two disciples begin to follow Jesus who turns and asks what they are looking for, to which they respond by calling Jesus "'Rabbi' (which is translated 'Teacher')" (1:38). Although this appellation is a relatively limited one given the overall Christology of the Fourth Gospel,[16] it is not insignificant that the idea of discipleship governs Jesus' relationship with his followers, rather than the idea of apostleship. The relationship implied is that between a teacher (Rabbi) and his students who seek the teacher out to learn and live a particular way of life constituted by attachment to the teacher.[17]

One of the two following Jesus is Andrew, who finds his brother Simon (Peter) and gossips: "We have found the Messiah (which is translated 'Christ')" (1:41). This face-to-face encounter involves ascribing Jesus, with the honorific title "Messiah." The generative cause of this gossip event is unclear, but related to the disciples' stay with Jesus "that day" (1:39). Indeed, the verbs "abiding" (*menō*) and "follow" (*akoloutheō*) imply an exclusive loyalty to Jesus on the part of these two former disciples of John the Baptist.[18] Moreover, the title "Messiah," a title refused by the Baptist, is greater than that of "Rabbi" (1:38) and thus, reflects how the two disciples' understanding of Jesus' identity has changed. In short, the results of the two disciples following and abiding with Jesus is the beginning of the formation of Jesus' fictive kin-group, and the further construction of Jesus' identity—Jesus the Rabbi, is Messiah. The ascription of Jesus as "Messiah" is significant. To begin with, it is a title that

15. Malina and Rohrbaugh, *Gospel of John*, 49–50; Neyrey and Rohrbaugh, "He Must Increase."

16. Moloney, *Gospel of John*, 60.

17. Malina and Rohrbaugh, *Gospel of John*, 48; Keener, *Gospel of John*, 1:468.

18. Malina and Rohrbaugh, *Gospel of John*, 55.

never emerges from Jesus' lips in the Fourth Gospel. Indeed, Jesus is ascribed by this gossip as the man (human being) anointed by God to help God establish God's rule at the end of time.[19] Moreover, it is also striking that at two places in John the title "Messiah" is associated with components of a shamanic figure (cf. 4:29; 11:27).[20]

The next gossip event happens again, on "the next day" (*tē epaurion*; 1:43) when Jesus calls Philip to follow him, resulting in Philip not only following, but seeking out others to do so as well. Philip finds Nathanael and gossips about Jesus: "We have found the one whom Moses wrote about in the Law as well as the prophets, Jesus son of Joseph, from Nazareth" (1:45). Philip's gossip, apparently positive, carries a note of ambivalence since the initial ascription of Jesus' identity as the subject of Hebrew prophecy is immediately tempered by the details of his lineage from Joseph of Nazareth. Unlike the previous two gossip events wherein the information is passively received by the hearers, Nathanael responds by undercutting Philip's initial assertion: "So, Nathanael said to him, 'Is it possible for anything good to come out of Nazareth?'" (1:46). The information conveyed by Philip, simultaneously builds on Jesus' in-group identity while creating tension since the one prophesied by Moses and "the prophets" is also of the rather mundane lineage of a peasant village artisan. Philip is portrayed seeing Jesus in terms of geographical stereotyping and familial reputation. The reader is aware of the tension given the prologue's appraisal of Jesus' origin from God (1:1) as well as his identity as the "only Son" of God (1:18). Nathanael's stereotypical response underscores that being the son of Joseph of Nazareth is not indicative of honorable repute.

The tension created around Jesus' identity with this gossip event is remarkable. On offer here are both positive and negative appraisals as individuals adjudicate the identity of Jesus, the leader of an emerging faction. This sort of adjudicative gossip happens a number of times in this gospel (e.g., 7:12; 10:20-21) and little effort

19. Ashton, *Understanding the Fourth Gospel*, 255.

20. The Samaritan woman's gossip about Jesus is generated by his divine knowledge about her life, and is comparable to Jesus' knowledge about Nathanael. And at 11:27, Martha calls Jesus "Messiah" and "Son of God," thus associating the two titles and implying the shamanic indicator of divine sonship.

is made to release the tension such talk engenders. In any event, the tension between Nathanael and Jesus is somewhat relieved by the emphasis on his prophetic power ("I saw you under the fig tree"; 1:48) that leads to Nathanael's identifying Jesus as "Rabbi," "Son of God," and "King of Israel" (1:49). This identification betrays Nathanael's knowledge of the righteous Messianic branch (see Zech 3:8–10; Jer 23:5; 33:15), and thus makes further sense of Jesus' response to him as a guileless Israelite who will soon see the glory of God made manifest.[21]

Jesus responds to Nathanael with the promise of a vision: "Truly I say to you, you will see the heaven opened and the angels of God ascending and descending on the Son of Man" (1:51). Such a response prefaced with "truly I say to you" is formulaic for the Fourth Gospel, occurring twenty times, and signaling when Jesus is about to say something important. Moreover, Jesus' apparent self-awareness of his own origins compels his authoritative speech describing what amounts to a shamanic ASC experience.[22] The opening of the heaven can be seen in light of the Baptist's ASC of Jesus' spirit-possession thus, filling out details left out by the Evangelist that would be equivalent to Synoptic baptisms.[23] The second element of the vision describing the angels of God going up and down on the Son of Man are crucial to the text's connection to Genesis 28:12, where Jacob sees a ladder stretching between the earth and heaven with angels going up and down. Thus, the entire scene (1:47–51) in fact, describes the newness of Jesus' movement within Israel. Nathanael represents Israel, seeing that the pronouns "you" are plural in 1:51, though without the guile of Jacob (1:47; see also Gen 27), who will witness the imminent cosmic transformation the likes of which are usually attended by angels.[24] The vision is similar to Jacob's: "And he dreamed that there was a ladder set up on earth, the top of it reaching to heaven; and the angels of God were ascending and descending on it. And the Lord said, 'I am the

---

21. Koester, "Messianic Exegesis," 30–31.
22. Craffert, *Life*, 344.
23. Brown, *Gospel According to John*, 91.
24. Gomes, "John 1:45–51," 286.

Lord, the God of Abraham your father and the God of Isaac'" (Gen 28:12-13a). The vision Jesus promises Nathanael envisages the attending angels going up and coming down not on a ladder, but on the Son of Man. In other words, Jesus is asserting himself as the Son of Man who is the "locus of divine glory" and the "point of contact between heaven and earth."[25]

Indeed, Craffert suggests that Son of Man sayings in the gospels are linked to distinct features of a shamanic figure including experiences being a mediator of power and knowledge, self-understanding as a mediator figure, as well as to cultural dynamics of a shamanic figure such as a divine agent, broker, or entrepreneur.[26] In other words, when Jesus talked about himself as Son of Man, he was talking about his own shamanic experiences that impacted and affirmed his identity.[27] Keener sums it up well in language that clearly articulates characteristics normally associated with a shamanic figure:

> Jesus is the link between heaven and earth, the realms above and below, between God and humanity, throughout his entire ministry as he later explains to Nathanael's friend Philip (14:9). . . . Thus, he is not only the "Son of Man" who will come from heaven (Dan 7:13-14), but is the mediator between heaven and earth, on whom the angels must travel. . . . In short, Jesus is Jacob's ladder, the one who mediates between God in heaven and his servant Jacob on earth.[28]

Alternatively, O'Neill follows Jeremias in understanding the verb "come down" (*katabainō*) with the preposition "upon" (*epi*) plus the accusative "Son of Man" (*ton huion tou anthrōpou*) at John 1:51 to call for translating the preposition "unto" rather than "on," thus moving away from Barrett's understanding of "Son of Man" replacing the ladder in Jacob's dream.[29] This is significant for seeing the Son of Man as the place on earth from which and to which the

---

25 Brown, *Gospel According to John*, 91.
26 Craffert, *Life*, 348.
27 Ibid., 349.
28 Keener, *Gospel of John*, 1:489.
29 O'Neill, "Son of Man," 375; See also Barrett, *Gospel According to St. John*, 187.

angels ascend and descend. Indeed, O'Neill agrees with Jeremias's suggestion that the Son of Man was the very stone at Bethel in the story, the very place of the presence of God, the house of God, and door to heaven (Gen 28:17, 22).[30] O'Neill's description is as appropriate as Keener's for construing a shamanic figure:

> Where he was, the presence of God was; where he was, there was the gate of heaven; where he was there the spirits of God were standing ready to serve and to bring the bread of life, the living word of God, down to earth.[31]

In sum, Jesus is further ascribed as a shamanic figure by adjudicative gossip about his identity which in this case, is settled by means of Nathanael's re-ascription of Jesus in terms associated with a shamanic figure in light of a demonstration of divine knowledge, and Jesus' self-ascription as the Son of Man.

FROM INSIDERS TO OUTSIDERS

Through John 2:1—4:54, the Evangelist turns from the construction of Jesus by members of his emerging group to that of outsiders. It is significant that this occurs after the commencement of Jesus' signs beginning with his turning water into wine at a wedding in Cana of Galilee (2:1–11). The miraculous deeds, or "signs," in the Fourth Gospel function to reveal the person of Jesus and are thus an intricate aspect of the Christology of John, not only calling people to faith in Jesus, but interpreting his identity as well.[32] The newness

---

30. O'Neill, "Son of Man," 377.
31. Ibid., 377.
32. Brown, *Gospel According to John*, 103; Barrett, *Gospel According to St. John*, 75; Keener, *Gospel of John*, 1:275. For a literary perspective on the signs as "recognition scenes," see Larsen, *Recognizing the Stranger*. Larsen's work deftly recognizes the complexity of Jesus' construction in the prologue, seeing Jesus as a "hybrid" character that bears both "marks" pointing to his identity, and "flesh" concealing his identity. It is this dynamic, Larsen adds, that eventually leads to debates about Jesus' identity among various characters in the narrative, and usually outsiders. In the parlance of the Social Sciences, what Larsen is getting at is the social process of challenge-riposte and its role in identity construction. See also Culpepper, "Cognition in John"; Kim, "Significance" and "Christological and Eschatological Significance."

implied in Jesus' promised vision to Nathanael (1:51) is fortified by Jesus' signs the Evangelist connects with the "New Exodus" theme portraying Jesus as a figure greater than Moses—a detail of some significance for gossip encountered in John 6 (cf. 3:14; 5:45–47; 6:32; 9:28).[33] In any event, Jesus' signs turn out to be a catalyst for much of the gossip in the Fourth Gospel that constructs his identity from the perspective of outsiders (cf. 1:10–11). This construction, of course, stands in stark contrast to that of the readers (1:14), Jesus' insiders, and those who at least recognize him partially. We move through this section first dealing with a text that implies some assessment of the topic of gossip (2:23–24) before moving to texts embodying the process (3:22–30; 4:1–42).

Johannine Assessment of Gossip: John 2:23–24

John 2:23–24 not only offers commentary on Jesus' assessment of faith based on signs, but also an important appraisal of the information transacted over the gossip network. Following the first sign in Cana, and the "cleansing of the Temple" (2:13–22), the narrator reports that Jesus was in Jerusalem during Passover and that many people were believing in his name precisely because of his signs. The detail that many people believed because of what they saw draws a connection between faith and experience that in turn, suggests the cultural plausibility of what is described. Moreover, since gossip is involved in the initial construction of events—"What did he say?" "What did he do?"—experiencing Jesus' signs, and sharing the experiences with others via the gossip network, also contributes to his social identity. This understanding is reinforced by comparing 2:23–25 with 3:2 where Nicodemus offers his report from the grapevine: "Rabbi, we know that you are a teacher who has come from God; for no one can do these signs that you do apart from the presence of God." Nicodemus's report of the gossip network confirms Jesus' teachings are connected to his signs, and are construed to indicate a close connection between him and God.[34] Eventually,

---

33. Keener, *Gospel of John*, 1:271.
34. Craffert, *Life*, 338, 348.

the knowledge about Jesus that Nicodemus holds on to proves to be inadequate. Similarly, the signs for which the many are following Jesus at 2:23–25, although spreading information about Jesus, result in Jesus not trusting them. Thus, what we have here is a tacit negative construal of gossip on the part of the Fourth Evangelist.

Within Israel: John 3:22–30

After a private meeting with Nicodemus at night, Jesus and his disciples are reported entering the Judean countryside. Interestingly, we are informed that Jesus was baptizing near where John the Baptist was also baptizing (3:22–23). After a discussion about purification emerges between John's disciples and a Judean, the narrative reports that they all came to John and began to gossip about Jesus baptizing: "Rabbi, the one who was with you across the Jordan, to whom you testified, here he is baptizing, and all are going to him" (3:26). At first glance, the statement does not appear to be evaluative, and is thus, lacking one of the principle criteria for gossip. However, considering the social dynamics of group identity, it becomes apparent that the statement is encoded with negative evaluation—Jesus' group has invaded the space of the Baptist's group, and is doing something that stands as a pivotal identity marker for the Baptist's group, that is, baptizing. In other words, the incursion onto the Baptist's territory, both spatially and in terms of activity, is an assault on the very identity of the Baptist's group, centered as it is, around a prophetic figure known as "the dunker." In the agonistic world of the text, the words of "the Judean" reporting how "all are going to Jesus," implies that Jesus has challenged the Baptist in an attempt to gain reputation and status.[35]

The Baptist's response to this negative gossip about Jesus is astonishing. Indeed, his response is in keeping with his function as a witness to Jesus ascribed to him early on (1:6–8, 15, 19–34): "No one can receive anything except what has been given from heaven. You yourselves are my witnesses that I said 'I am not the Messiah,

---

35. Neyrey, *Gospel of John*, 84; Neyrey and Rohrbaugh, "He Must Increase," 466.

but I have been sent ahead of him.' . . . He must increase, but I must decrease" (3:27-28, 30). John, apparently unconcerned with the challenge implied by Jesus' actions, deflates his own disciples' envy by suggesting Jesus' gain is not his own, but rather, ascribed to him "from heaven" (3:27).[36] Since the divine benefaction comes from God, the Baptist has no concern over the loss or gain of honor, and even joyfully subordinates himself—as a friend subordinates himself to a bridegroom (3:29)—to Jesus.

The content of the gossip generated by Jesus' baptizing, associates him with the ancient Jewish practice and ascribes the activity to Jesus' social-identity. The previous scenario with Nicodemus highlights this: "Very truly, I tell you, no one can enter the kingdom of God without being born of water and Spirit" (3:5). In fact, the entirety of the peculiar conversation between Nicodemus and Jesus revolves around baptism which is the subject of Jesus' heavenly speech that goes misunderstood. Such birth "from above" (3:3) associates baptism with the ASC experience of Jesus as God's Son who comes "from above,"[37] thus, embodying the heavenly speech of Jesus in the practice of baptism (3:26). It seems clear that Jesus is here associated closely with an important feature of the shamanic complex since this story, and the other baptism stories in the Synoptics all contain important elements of shamanic initiation including ASCs, soul flights and sky journeys (inferring Jesus' origins "from above"), and spirit-possession.[38]

Without Israel: John 4:1-42

The story of the Samaritan woman through John 4:1-42 is one of a number of complex discourses between Jesus and an individual which the Evangelist uses to underscore both Jesus' origins from the heavens (3:3) and to disclose the potential a person "of this

---

36. Neyrey, *Gospel of John*, 85.

37. Malina and Rohrbaugh, *Social-Science Commentary on the Gospel of John*, 83.

38. Craffert, *Life*, 217; see also Eliade, *Shamanism*, 33-144; Smith, *Jesus the Magician*, 104; Ashton, *Religion of Paul*, 62-72.

world" has to grow in knowledge/faith, and eventually become a member of Jesus' group. Some grow in knowledge and faith, and so become insiders, while others apparently do not (e.g., the lame man at 5:2–15; Pontius Pilate at 18:28–38). Still others, respond to Jesus ambivalently (Nicodemus, 3:1–15; see also 7:50–51; 19:39–40). Although the status of the woman in relation to Jesus' group by the end of the chapter remains mysterious, it is not of little importance that even someone who does not know fully who Jesus is, can bring an entire village to full knowledge. The Samaritan woman's final response to Jesus stands in relief to Nicodemus's as she is able to engage Jesus in substantive discourse, although their conversation bears some ambiguities similar to Jesus' encounter with Nicodemus. However, unlike Nicodemus, the Samaritan woman does not walk away from Jesus confounded at the strangeness of his words.

Scholars have for some time noticed the exchange between the Samaritan woman and Jesus can be divided into two sections, 4:7–15 and 4:16–26.[39] The first part is unique since the woman's misunderstanding is the catalyst for the discussion. The second section describes the details of a zesty discourse, which is followed by gossip. Before looking closely at the gossip encountered in the narrative, a number of details about the socio-cultural framework are worth mentioning. First, the story of the encounter between Jesus and the woman implies the agonistic backdrop for nearly every public meeting between two persons from different groups in Mediterranean antiquity. Jesus is an insider to the larger "Judean" group as the woman is to the Samaritans, so that they are both "outsiders" to each other. Additionally, since geographical stereotyping probably scripted how both Samaritans and Judeans acted around each other, the two likely anticipate what to expect from each other in this encounter. The woman's response to Jesus' request for water betrays that neither likely expects much from the other in this encounter: "How is it that you, a Jew, ask a drink of me a woman of Samaria?" (4:9). As things unfold however, what they both get from each other is remarkable.

---

39. O'Day, *Word Disclosed*, 39, 46; Neyrey, *Gospel of John*, 89; Moloney, *Gospel of John*, 115, 126.

Gossiping Jesus Within and Without Israel

The fact that Jesus' dialogue partner here is both a Samaritan and a woman is culturally overshadowed by the belief that such a one was unclean "from the cradle."[40] So, to any observers, let alone the readers of the Fourth Gospel, issues surrounding purity were at play. A woman alone in public space with a man who is not either her husband or head of her household/group was problematic given the cultural notions of sexuality.[41] The Mediterranean culture also prescribed that women belonged and operated in private space (the home), while men belonged and operated in public space.[42] This corresponds with the idea that honor was transacted by men in public, while shame was (positively) maintained and managed by women in private space.[43] Indeed, in antiquity, and even today, many Mediterranean women create private space by wearing a veil in public. In any event, Neyrey, summarizes the awkward, even volatile socio-cultural situation describing the woman as the "ultimate outsider" since she is female, apparently shameless (due to numerous husbands), unclean, and a Samaritan.[44]

The interaction takes an interesting turn when the woman engages Jesus in a game of challenge-riposte (4:16–26), given that such a process normally only occurred between men in public.[45] Most striking is the final riposte (of four exchanges) resulting in Jesus clearly revealing he is the Messiah to the woman with the words "I am" (*egō eimi*) which is the Fourth Gospel's major claim for Jesus' identity (8:24, 28, 58; 13:19; 18:5) that moreover, corresponds with the Divine name revealed to Moses and reflected on by the prophets (Exod 3:14; Isa 43:10; 45:18). In other words, the woman's positive challenge to Jesus is ultimately responded to rewardingly with a revelation of his identity.

40. *m. Nid.* 4:1.
41. Malina, *Social World*, 48–51.
42. Malina and Rohrbaugh, *Social-Science Commentary on the Gospel of John*, 104–5.
43. Malina, *New Testament World*, 44–47.
44. Neyrey, *Gospel of John*, 94–95.
45. Crook has shown that, although not the norm, women were imagined in some of the literature to publicly challenge men. See "Honor, Shame, and Social Status Revisited," 604–9.

The two-part discussion entails a series of "testimonies" on the woman's part to Jesus' identity, each testimony reflecting her advancing knowledge of Jesus. From the start the woman is an outsider who perceives Jesus in earthly categories the way any individual "of this world" might, namely, as a "Judean" who oddly asked her for a drink (4:9). Soon after the encounter, the woman is bearing witness to Jesus gossiping about him to the people of Sychar: "Come and see a man who told me everything I have ever done! He cannot be the Messiah, can he?" (4:29). The content of this gossip is evaluative positively as it ascribes to an absent Jesus divine knowledge and the possible title of "Messiah." The use of the negative adverb "not" (*mēti*; translated "cannot be" in the NRSV) functions here to anticipate a negative response to the question. In other words, the Samaritan woman does not think Jesus is "Messiah," and so her gossip about Jesus is ambivalent in nature. The generative cause of her gossip is Jesus' prophetic ability to know how many husbands she actually has had, hence her construal that Jesus is a prophet (4:17–19). Therefore, the gossip event here is adjudicative since Jesus' identity is under construction in the content of the woman's speech itself, that is, her wondering out loud about who Jesus is, or is not. Moreover, her gossip associates Jesus' divine knowledge with another important element of the shamanic complex, namely, spirit possession which was presumed of a prophetic figure.[46]

Johannine Assessment of Gendered Gossip?

It was suggested earlier that John 2:23–25 may embody at least a tacit, negative assessment of gossip reflecting the prevailing opinion in antiquity. The words of the people from Sychar to the woman, after they come to believe in Jesus, may account for another clue to what the author of the Fourth Gospel thought about gossip. The social and cultural complexities of the entire narrative (4:1–42) are highly charged given the woman's gender, outsider status at first meeting Jesus, and her publicly delivered report to the people of

---

46. Although, in Jesus' case, it is the spirit of God that is presumed to possess him; see Craffert, *Life*, 228–29.

Sychar presumably in the village square which was "male space." So, the woman does not go to her socially prescribed private space,[47] her home, to relate her experience with Jesus. Instead, she simply went to "the city" and spoke to "the people" (4:29). Despite the woman's inadequate knowledge of Jesus' identity, the Evangelist avers her ascription of him as a prophet results in many Samaritans believing in Jesus: "Many Samaritans from the city believed in him because of the woman's testimony, 'He told me everything I have ever done'" (4:39). Then, after encountering Jesus themselves, the "many more" who believe "because of his word" (*logon*; 4:41), turn to the Samaritan woman and say: "It is no longer because of what you said that we believe, for we have heard for ourselves, and we know that this is truly the Savior of the world" (4:42). The shift in vocabulary for the woman's speech by the Evangelist is crucial. At 4:39 it is clear the Samaritan town believes because of the woman's "word," or *logon* in Greek. At 4:41, many more Samaritans believed on account of Jesus' "word," also *logon* in Greek. But when they turn to the woman to inform her of the new basis of their belief (Jesus' *logon*), they do it with words suggesting they are labeling the woman a "gossip": "It is no longer because of your word" (*lalian* in Greek). Interestingly, *lalian* is a word in antiquity often associated negatively with gossip.[48] Subsequently, this element of the story may bear the residue of negative female gendering of such speech.[49] However, since it is the Samaritans from Sychar themselves, in John's story-world, who label the woman's speech, it is quite possible the Evangelist is simply offering a believable portrait of first-century, primarily male bias toward women's speech.

---

47. Where large numbers of people assembled in the "open air" was suitable for men. But "women are best suited to the indoor life which never strays from the house." Philo, *Special Laws*, 3:169, cited in Malina and Rohrbaugh, *Social-Science Commentary on the Gospel of John*, 105.

48. 1 Tim 5:13; Rohrbaugh, *New Testament*, 136; and Moloney, *Gospel of John*, 147; Cf. Barrett, *Gospel According to St. John*, 243.

49. See Kartzow, "Female Gossipers"; and *Gossip and Gender*.

4

Gossiping Jesus on the Sabbath and Passover

John 5–6

AT THE FEASTS OF THE JUDEANS: JOHN 5:1—10:42

THIS SECTION IS ORGANIZED around a number of festivals—Sabbath (5:1–47), Passover (6:4–71), Tabernacles (7:2—8:59), the "last day" of Tabernacles (9:1—10:21), and Dedication (10:22–42)—and is rife with growing tension between Jesus and "the Judeans," signaled at John 5:6, and ranging from simple caution to outright opposition. The section describes a collision of horizons in the experience and celebration of the presence of God in the festivals, with Jesus saying things and observing festival in ways that emphasize his role as mediator between God and Israel (see 5:46–47; 6:32–33, 48–51). The social conflict is embodied in a series of challenges launched at Jesus and his group by rival groups intent on dishonoring them. The number of adjudicative gossip events in this part of the Fourth Gospel is surprising, with most resulting in a division among Jesus' opponents. Thus, the identity of Jesus is ambiguous, or rather, "under construction" from the standpoint of outsiders. Additionally, several of the gossip events are associated with the social process of challenge-riposte and the transaction of honor and/or shame.

Breaking the Sabbath: John 5:2–18

The story of Jesus healing a paralytic at John 5:2–18 is rather opaque compared to other narratives in John that describe Jesus encountering an individual. Here we have no prolonged, multilayered discourse, and no apparent knowledge or faith development on the part of the man healed. But, it is precisely this last point the story seeks to emphasize and even while offering ingredients for the construction of Jesus' identity, at least on the part of outsiders.

Knowing the paralytic had been lying next to the pool for a long time, Jesus asks the man, "Do you want to be made well?" (5:6). As if not hearing Jesus' question, the sick man complains about having no one to put him into the pool when the water is stirred (5:7). Because of this and his eventual tattling on Jesus to the Judeans (5:11), some interpreters are quick to characterize the man as lazy, self-pitying, and passive.[1] But, the paralytic's complaints reflect the seriousness of his situation. From a social scientific perspective, the man's complaint that he has no companions to help him into the water realistically implies the social dynamics involved with sin that likely resulted in separation from his primary group. The paralytic's situation is indeed, serious, since he is on his own.[2]

The paralytic's social circumstance is dire on several levels and is likely to get worse if he continues to isolate himself by sinning, presumably, against his primary relations (5:14). In Jesus' time, sinning was understood as an act of dishonoring or shaming both God, whose law had been broken, and the person(s) harmed by the trespass. In other words, not only was one's status as an Israelite strained, but the social relationship between the perpetrator

---

1. E.g., Talbert, *Reading John*, 122; and Culpepper, *Gospel and Letters*, 150–51.

2. Malina and Rohrbaugh, *Social-Science Commentary on the Gospel of John*, 111; Pilch, *Healing*, 128.

and victim damaged too. On the one hand, dishonoring God and neighbor triggered the defense of God's honor by the exercise of God's wrath, often in the form of illness.[3] On the other hand, since trespassing against God's Law meant trespassing against one's neighbors, friends, or kinfolk, the result would entail social consequences like that of the paralytic who subsequently, had no one to help him into the pool (5:7).

Such a complex notion of illness emerges from an ancient worldview wherein body, mind, and culture are not distinct or unconnected entities, but rather quite intricately related:

> If the human organism is viewed as composed of a number of hierarchically organized subsystems (particles, molecules, cells, organs) and itself belonging to larger systems (family, group, organization, society, nation, ecological environment), with each system relating reciprocally to others, health will be understood as a dynamic balance of the systems and illness as a disequilibrium.[4]

So, there is much more implied in the entire situation narrated in 5:1–9a than merely a paralyzed man being cured by Jesus. In the high-context culture of the first-century Mediterranean, sickness was experienced on several levels that included the physical, psychical, and the social. This is what social scientists have called the biopsychosocial framework[5] that effectively takes into consideration the overall experience of illness—it's biological, psychological, and social aspects—and thus makes good sense of the ancient idea of the relationship between deeds and consequences in the form of some physical malady. The man's sin has resulted in his being cut off from his primary group, with the result that he's left alone by the pool. The ancient Israelite notion of punishment in the here and now is being worked out in the paralytic's experience.

The gossip described in John 5:11–12 is generated by both Jesus' healing the paralytic, and the man's carrying his mat (5:9a), and both of these on the Sabbath (5:9b). The Judeans are the ones who,

3. Malina and Pilch, *Social-Science Commentary on the Letters of Paul*, 408–9.
4. Craffert, *Life*, 262.
5. Ibid., 260–99.

seeing the man walking alone with his mat in hand, point out the unlawfulness of his action (5:10; cf. Exod 20:8-11; Jer 17:19-27). The healed man in turn, points out that it was Jesus who both healed him, and instructed him to carry his mat on the Sabbath: "The man who made me well said to me, 'Take up your mat and walk.'" (5:11). Although this response to the Judeans' correction for carrying a bundle seems straightforward, it is seen here as constituting gossip since it is evaluative in nature, implying that "the man who made me well" was breaking the Sabbath and is subsequently responsible for the healed man's trespass. The Judeans respond with a question inquiring about Jesus' identity, thus inviting social construal of Jesus (5:12). The gossip is then concluded after the healed man encounters Jesus who again offers him sound advice to avoid worsening his already bereft situation (5:14). This time the man associates Jesus' name with the healing on the Sabbath (5:15), so that Jesus is now, as far as the man and the Judeans are concerned, a sinner (see also John 9:24b). The Judeans then persecute Jesus for healing on the Sabbath (5:16) and eventually seek to kill him because "he was not only breaking the Sabbath, but was also calling God his own Father, thereby making himself equal to God" (5:18).

Various words for healing are associated with Jesus in the Synoptics some fifty times.[6] Conversely, in John's gospel Jesus is portrayed healing a mere three times (4:46-54; 5:1-18; 9). But in all three instances, gossip is somehow involved in the story. This makes vividly clear the connection between the experience of healing from the perspective of both eyewitnesses to healing, and those healed. Indeed, from early on in John's narrative, Jesus' growing reputation can be accounted for given the healthy gossip network described (cf. 1:35-46; 2:23; 3:2; 4:28, 47; 6:2; etc.), and so there is little doubt that healing was becoming a constituent part of Jesus' social identity.

At this point it will be helpful to consider how this recollection of Jesus healing the paralytic constitutes Jesus as a shamanic figure. As the story demonstrates, gossip is intricate to the process of ascribing Jesus' identity. What this suggests at least, is the importance

---

6. Pilch, *Healing*, 119.

of gossip for *processing* the historical Jesus' identity. In other words, the gossip network conveys information about Jesus' effectiveness as a healer in a mode of speech that simultaneously constructs the healing event as a real cultural event, *and* constructs Jesus as a particular social personage. Associating Jesus with healing abilities, the gossip network provides both the vitality behind such oral reports that in turn, motivates the healing by nurturing and communicating Jesus' reputation as a healer, as well as the symbol behind him as a powerful healer.[7] Viewing Jesus' healings within the context of the shamanic complex, and thus associating him with a variety of other features and functions of a shamanic figure, this healing and others like it in John, can be seen as clues to how Jesus was experienced as a shamanic figure who healed often. Indeed, another feature of the shamanic complex involved here is Jesus' divine knowledge that the paralytic had been by the pool for a very long time.

Interestingly, even more than the healing itself, a detail that drives the bulk of the story, and sets up the lengthy discourse at 5:19–47, is the fact that Jesus healed on the Sabbath (5:9b). Given that a wandering shamanic figure would likely drift toward rural communities that gathered in synagogues, it is no surprise that many of Jesus' activities including healing, would likely occur in such Sabbath-gathering scenarios (Mark 3:1–6; Luke 13:10–17; John 9:1–12).[8] Thus, since Jesus was raised in the rural, Galilean peasant culture, he would likely have held a view of the cultic proscriptions in Torah differently from the Torah-keeping Judeans, and certainly different than the Pharisees. In fact, the depiction of Jesus arguing with authorities over Sabbath Law implies he was a master of the Lord's day, and thus, someone who could be ascribed as "Son of God."[9]

---

7. Craffert, *Life*, 296–97.
8. Ibid., 341.
9. Ibid.

The Bread of Life at Passover: John 6

By the time one gets to the sixth chapter of John's gospel, the hostility directed at Jesus has become acute since the radical turn taken at 5:18 mentioned earlier. To be sure, Jesus' description of his healing as God's work (on the Sabbath) is enough to reap the accusation of blasphemy from the Judeans. The gossip about Jesus in chapter 6 (6:14, 41–42, 52, 60) is either positive or negative, and couched amidst the growing hostility. So, the gossip takes on a more aggressive quality, and is in fact, used as a weapon of sorts to challenge Jesus' honor claims implied by his words and deeds.

A Prophet and a King

The story of Jesus feeding five thousand at John 6:1–15 is prefaced by a report of his growing reputation because of his miraculous signs carried by the gossip network (6:2). The first time the Evangelist describes Jesus' growing reputation and following as the result of his miraculous deeds, the reader is cued to be suspicious of faith based on such deeds (2:23–24). So, again, the reader is here cued to expect little, if anything good to result from the Jesus' ensuing encounter with the people. Jesus performs the sign while "up the mountain" (6:3); a detail evincing a comparison between himself and Moses who received the Torah on the mountain (Exod 19:20; 14:1–2) and who led the Israelites through the wilderness where God provided manna from heaven (Exod 16:8, 12, 16, 18, 21). This is supported by the fact that there was a surplus left over for the disciples to "gather up" (*sunagō*; 6:12), a gathering reminiscent of the gathering up of manna by the Israelites in the wilderness (Exod 16:16), except the wilderness gathering faded away (Exod 16:21). Such a comparison implies what has been hinted at all along in the gospel's narrative, namely, that Jesus surpasses both Moses, and what Moses provided by means of the Torah.

The multiplication of the loaves and fish is one of Jesus' signs that generates gossip among "the people" (*hoi anthrōpoi*) who witnessed it and, subsequently, began to construe both the event and Jesus' identity and origins: "This is indeed the prophet who is to come into the world" (6:14). This is face-to-face gossip amongst a group of people about a third party subject who is present. What is not clear is whether Jesus hears the gossip or not, although his knowledge of the group's intentions implies he may have been aware that they were gossiping about him (6:15). In any case, the gossip is positive in character, ascribing to Jesus the acclamation that he is "the prophet who is to come into the world" (see 1:21, 45; 4:19), and perhaps, in light of Deuteronomy 18:15 and following, the Messiah himself.[10]

Bread that Came Down from Heaven

After feeding five thousand and evading the people intent on taking him forcibly and making him king (6:15), the story relates the episode of Jesus walking on water. Although certainly describing Jesus as a shamanic figure, in terms of such a figure's ability to control nature, this detail places Jesus on the other side of the sea, away from the crowd, which of course, leads to "the crowd" (*ho ochlos*) pursuing Jesus, that is quite literally, "seeking after" (*zēteō*; 6:22–24) which, in light of 5:18, suggests they intend to do him harm. When the crowd finds Jesus, they immediately issue a challenge that initiates a series of challenge-ripostes.[11]

> Challenge: When they found him on the other side of the sea, they said to him, "Rabbi, when did you come here? (6:25)
>
> Riposte: Jesus answered them, "Very truly, I tell you, you are looking for me, not because you saw signs, but because you ate your fill of the loaves. Do not work for the food that perishes, but for the food that endures for eternal life, which the Son of Man will give you. For it is on him that God the Father has set his seal." (6:26–27)
>
> Challenge: Then they said to him, "What must we do to perform the works of God?" (6:28)
>
> Riposte: Jesus answered them, "This is the work of God, that you believe in him whom he has sent." (6:29)

10. Barrett, *Gospel According to St. John*, 277.
11. Moloney, *Gospel of John*, 207–8.

Challenge: So they said to him, "What sign are you going to give us then, so that we may see it and believe you? What work are you performing? Our ancestors ate the manna in the wilderness; as it is written 'He gave them bread from heaven to eat.'" (6:30–31)

Riposte: Then Jesus said to them, "Very truly, I tell you, it was not Moses who gave you the bread from heaven, but it is my Father who gives you the true bread from heaven. For the bread of God is that which comes down from heaven and gives life to the world." (6:32–33)

Challenge: They said to him, "Sir, give us this bread always." (6:34)

Riposte: Jesus said to them, "I am the bread of life. Whoever comes to me will never be hungry, and whoever believes in me will never be thirsty. But I said to you that you have seen me and yet do not believe. Everything that the Father gives me will come to me, and anyone who comes to me I will never drive away; for I have come down from heaven, not to do my own will, but the will of him who sent me. And this is the will of him who sent me, that I should lose nothing of all that he has given me, but raise it up on the last day. This is indeed the will of the Father, that all who see the Son and believe in him may have eternal life; and I will raise them up on the last day." (6:35–40)

This text is remarkable given the vivid description of the crowd's agonistic reaction to Jesus' words and deeds. Being outsiders, they neither understand his words, nor can they host the situation that Jesus from Nazareth is able to multiply the loaves. This is exacerbated by the explicit suggestion that God provides Jesus, the "bread of God" from heaven, and this over-against Moses who was not even the one who provided the manna which spoils (6:32). Not only is Jesus superior compared to Moses, but also compared to the Torah since he is the "bread of life" "from heaven" which provides eternal life:

See, I have set before you today life and prosperity, death and adversity. (Gen 30:15)

Choose life so that you and your descendants may live, loving the LORD your God, obeying him, and holding fast to him;

for that means life to you and length of days, so that you may live in the land that the LORD swore to give to your ancestors, to Abraham, to Isaac, and to Jacob. (Deut 30:19b-20)

He bestowed knowledge upon them, and allotted to them the law of life. (Sir 17:11)

He allowed him to hear his voice, and led him into the dark cloud, and gave him the commandments face to face, the law of life and knowledge, so that he might teach Jacob the covenant, and Israel his decrees. (Sir 45:5)

This is indeed an important contrast between Jesus and Moses, the Bread of Life and manna in the wilderness, Jesus the food that gives life and Torah that does not. The contrasts provide the basis for the tension between Jesus and outsiders even while it illustrates the black and white mindset of an anti-society asserting its own innovation using anti-language that leaves those of the prevailing consensus confused.[12]

Jesus' words "I am the bread of life" at 6:35 are one of twenty-four emphatic "I am" (*egō eimi*) statements in the Fourth Gospel (e.g., 4:26; 6:20, 41, 48, 51; 8:12, 18, 23, 24, 28, 58; 10:7, 9, 11, 14; 11:25; etc.) that are all weighted with Christological significance.[13] Moreover, Jesus' claims that he is "the bread of life" (6:35), the "bread of God" come down from heaven (6:33, 38), is received by the Judeans with expected recalcitrance in the form of gossip:

Then the Jews began to complain about him because he said "I am the bread come down from heaven." And they were saying, "Is this not Jesus the son of Joseph whose father and mother we know? How can he now say, 'I have come down from heaven'"? (6:41-42)

Potentially leaders of the Capernaum synagogue (6:59), "the Judeans" here emerge out of the crowd and "complain" about Jesus because of his words. This translation of a verb (*gonguzō*) elsewhere rendered "murmur," is more descriptive of the character of their discourse rather than the kind of discourse. In other words, their

12. Malina and Rohrbaugh, *Social-Science Commentary on the Gospel of John*, 46-48.
13. Barrett, *Gospel According to St. John*, 291-93; Bultmann, *Gospel of John*, 225-26.

complaint comes in the form of gossip.[14] It is significant that the murmuring of "the Judeans" here recalls the same sort of speech uttered in the wilderness by the Israelites who "murmured" (*gonguzō* in the LXX; Exod 15:24; 16:2; 17:3) against Moses and God about the provision of sustenance (food!), and here in John's gospel underscores similar obduracy in the face of Jesus' Christological claims to be true sustenance that gives life (cf. 3:16, 36; 10:10). For the wandering Israelites it was manna, the angel's food (Wis 16:20), that sustained life, but for John it is Jesus.

In any event, this bit of gossip, third-person speech rendering a present Jesus "absent" from the discourse, is generated by Jesus' unusual words that are essentially honor claims based on his lineage and origin.[15] The Judeans respond with gossip challenging Jesus' assertions over his origin from the heavenly realm, and his lineage, claiming that they "know" (*oidamen*) Jesus' lineage, and that he thus, cannot come from heaven. The fact that the Judeans' challenge to Jesus' claims comes in the form of gossip is noticeable because not only is Jesus present, but the talk is intended to be publicly uttered for all present to hear, and thus, for the third-party subject to hear as well. Such discourse is common in both ancient and extant traditional Mediterranean cultures, and indeed in nearly every other culture as well.[16] In such instances, the subject, although actually present, is rendered absent by numerous strategies. In this case, third-person speech does the job.[17] If this sort of speech is indeed what is being described at John 6:42, this demonstrates a peculiar function of gossip within the framework of challenge-riposte. In other words, the Judeans challenge Jesus' claims implied by his strange words about his identity and origin as the bread of life from heaven (6:35-40), not by direct questions or counter-claims, but by gossiping about him so that he will overhear. Since everyone else present will certainly overhear the talk, as well

---

14. Rohrbaugh includes the verb *gonguzō* in his lexicon of vocabulary signaling gossip. *New Testament*, 136.

15. Malina and Rohrbaugh, *Social-Science Commentary on the Gospel of John*, 41-42.

16. Handelman, "Gossip in Encounters," 213.

17. Bergmann, *Discreet Indiscretions*, 79-80.

Gossiping Jesus on the Sabbath and Passover

as the social diminution culturally encoded in the talk, a response to the challenge from Jesus is expected. Thus, the challenge is laid – will Jesus respond, or not? And if so, how?

Jesus' response is up to the task and very direct as he chides the Judeans because of their gossip: "Do not complain among yourselves" (6:43).[18] Jesus then reasserts his honor claim by reaffirming his origins from the Father while emphasizing that it is the Father who draws people to him: "No one can come to me unless drawn by the Father who sent me" (6:44a). Thus, Jesus' honor claims are not fortified by earthly categories as the Judeans attempt to suggest, but by heavenly categories so that his claims are backed by the Father in heaven.[19]

Jesus then reasserts his identity as the bread of life (6:48) in a way emphasizing again the superiority of himself and what he offers, over Moses and the manna in the wilderness (6:49–51). Once again, Jesus' anti-language increases the tension: "I am the living bread that came down from heaven. Whoever eats of this bread will live forever; and the bread that I give for the life of the world is my flesh" (6:51). Such language, which makes sense to Jesus' group (but 6:60 below!), makes no sense to the Judeans who respond by disputing "among themselves" (*pros allēlous*): "How can this man give us his flesh to eat?" (6:52b). This inquisitive disputation of the Judeans "among themselves" constitutes gossip sharing the same theme of "murmuring" at 6:42 and evoking Exodus 16 again. Moreover, the talk stands as a further challenge to Jesus' words received by outsider Judeans as an absurd invitation to anthropophagy,[20] which becomes offensive by Jesus' exhorting the drinking of his blood; a notion explicitly forbidden by Torah (Gen 9:4; Lev 3:17; Deut 12:23). On the other hand, for members of Jesus' group, life that resides in the flesh and blood of Jesus is something more than

---

18. Again the NRSV translation of *gonguzō* distracts from the character of the discourse. Raymond Brown's translation is preferable: "Stop your murmuring." *Gospel*, 268. See also Malina and Rohrbaugh, *Social-Science Commentary on the Gospel of John*, 132.

19. Malina and Rohrbaugh, *Social-Science Commentary on the Gospel of John*, 134.

20. Bultmann, *Gospel*, 235.

a simple possession, but something to have in themselves (*echete zōēn en heautois*, 6:53).[21] For them, the demand to eat his flesh and drink his blood is an invitation to welcome, accept, receive, and believe in Jesus, so the language of eating Jesus' flesh even replaces conventional language signaling dyadic interrelatedness common to collectivistic group relations and membership.[22] Indeed, Jesus' words indicate as such: "Those who eat my flesh and drink my blood abide in me, and I in them" (6:56). The language of "abiding" (*menō*) is significant as it describes the relationship between the Father, Son, and Spirit (1:32–33; 14:10; 15:10), and implying the dyadic relationship of believers.[23]

Jesus' strange words about eating his flesh provoke public sanction. Jesus is labeled with respect to his lineage and origin by means of aggressive gossip intended to be overheard and thus, to intimidate. Jesus continues to speak in language intelligible only to his group so that the Judeans are bewildered much like Nicodemus was earlier (6:52; cf. 3:9).

Eating Flesh and Drinking Blood

When Jesus' words about eating his flesh and drinking his blood reach "many of his disciples" it evokes an exceptionally interesting and evaluative utterance: "This teaching is difficult; who can accept it?" (6:60). This gossip event is significant since it suggests that even apparent insiders, that is, members of Jesus' primary in-group, are not able to host the teachings of their leader. This is remarkable since such inability to accept Jesus' words is a characteristic response of outsiders, that is, those without faith who are not part of Jesus' group, and not that of insiders who should, in fact, know and accept Jesus' words.

---

21. Ibid.
22. Malina and Rohrbaugh, *Social-Science Commentary on the Gospel of John*, 234–35; Moloney, *Gospel of John*, 222.
23. Carson, *Gospel*, 298; Smith, *John*, 159; Barrett, *Gospel According to St. John*, 299; Bultmann, *Gospel*, 236.

The narrator makes clear Jesus is aware of his disciples' gossip (*gonguzō*) and thus, responds to it: "Does this offend you?" (6:61). His response indicates the disciples may have intended Jesus to overhear their gossip, and thus, embody a particularly mordant challenge to Jesus' words. If this is correct, what we have described here is mutiny on the part of many disciples challenging their leader because of his words. Jesus' riposte is itself a counter-challenge recalling his identity and origin as the *unique revelation* of God from heaven (identity), and as the Son of Man *from* heaven (origin; 6:62). In other words, if Jesus' coming down from heaven (origin), along with his words of revelation cause outsiders to stumble, how much more will his going back up (resurrection/ascension) to heaven, his place of origin, cause them to stumble. Jesus' counter-challenge recalls his words to Nicodemus (3:13) that the Son of Man has come down from heaven. This implies then, that the disciples will see him going back up, as was the case with the ascent of other revealers like Abraham, Moses, Isaiah, and Enoch.[24] The result of Jesus' rejoinder is the loss of a number of his followers (6:66).

Turning to those who remain, Jesus issues a challenge to their group loyalty while expecting a negative response: "Do you also wish to go away?" (6:67). In sharp contrast to the "many disciples," Peter testifies not only to Jesus' identity, but to his (Peter's) and the remaining disciples' enduring loyalty to the group: "Lord, to whom can we go? You have the words of eternal life. We have come to believe and know that you are the Holy One of God" (6:68–69). But Peter's testimony is unsettled by Jesus' response that rather than lauding Peter for the truth of his rather robust testimony, instead refocuses things on the imminent betrayal: "Did I not choose you, the twelve? Yet one of you is a devil" (6:70). Jesus' words are ominous as they threaten the very foundation of his group, namely, their collective loyalty to his program. The threat is poignant since Jesus himself chose the twelve, and yet, one of his hand-picked is capable of betrayal (cf. 1:46; 4:33; 6:7–9; 9:2).

Four gossip events constitute the dynamic sixth chapter of John, all of which are generated by Jesus' words and deeds. All of the gossip conveys or implies interesting construals of Jesus' identity

---

24. Moloney, *Gospel of John*, 228.

as that identity is suggested by "the people" ("the prophet who is to come into the world"), and the Evangelist remembering Jesus as a teacher of new knowledge that is ironically reinforced by the challenging gossip of both the Judeans (6:41–42, 52) and some of Jesus' disciples (6:60). While the challenges from the Judeans, and peculiarly from "some of his disciples," reflect an outsider misunderstanding of Jesus' insider anti-language, Jesus' response to those challenges focuses on his superiority to Moses, his unique relationship with the Father, and his origins from above, that is, the major themes emphasized throughout the chapter. Not surprisingly, those aspects of Jesus' identity embodied in his words and deeds and reified by the gossip, are elements of the various features and functions of the shamanic complex that underscore Jesus' social identity as a shamanic figure.

5

Gossiping Jesus at Tabernacles
John 7-11

DISPUTATIOUS GOSSIP: JOHN 7

JOHN 7 MARKS A significant change of venue for Jesus, from Galilee to Judea. The conflict that emerges in chapter 5 (5:18!) and builds with the agonistic challenge-riposte between Jesus and the Judeans in chapter 6, peaks in the seventh which records the greatest number of gossip events (seven!) of all the chapters of the gospel (7:12, 15, 25-27, 31, 35-36, 40-44, 47-48). Certainly much of the tension can be attributed to the fact that Jesus is a Galilean in Judea, interacting with Judeans in stereotypical ways and with stereotypical expectations driven by mutual distrust of outsiders. Moreover, Jesus' insider anti-language continues to catalyze misunderstanding generating evaluative discourse as it did in chapter 6. Gossip is thus, quite believably embedded into this conflictive chapter as those who encounter Jesus struggle to make sense of his words and so, (re)construct the world in light of his words. The centrality of the social process is illustrated by the fact that schismatic gossip about Jesus' identity and origins is anchored in the story-world "about the middle of the feast" (7:14; 7:14-24, 25-31, 32-36).[1]

---

1. See the outline by Moloney, *Gospel of John*, 236.

Gossiping Jesus

What is particularly interesting about the gossip in this chapter is the fact that much of it is adjudicative in character with the discussants unable to reach a univocal appraisal of Jesus (7:11-12, 25-27, 40-44, 46-49). While this is to be expected given Jesus' destabilizing insider talk and the fact that he is an outsider, it is important to recall how such ambivalence in construing Jesus and his words is something that even insiders, that is, members of Jesus' group, are quite capable of as this was illustrated in the previous chapter (6:60-71). Another interesting feature is the variety of persons/groups the Evangelist identifies as engaging in evaluative talk about Jesus; "the crowds" (7:12), "the Judeans" (7:15, 35), "some of the people of Jerusalem" (7:25), "many in the crowd (who) believed in him" (7:31), "some in the crowd" (7:40), "others" in the crowd (7:41), "the police" (7:46), and "the Pharisees" (7:46). This offers a rather vivid portrait of an oral culture engaged in construing what are unexpected, and indeed strange words.

The first gossip scenario of the chapter is apparently generated by Jesus' absence from the festival, and is fueled by reports circulating about him via the gossip and rumor networks (7:3; see also 3:2; 2:23). While it is the Judeans who are looking for Jesus wondering where he is (7:11), it is among "the crowds" where there is "considerable complaining" (*gongusmos*; 7:12) about him. Significantly, the discourse here is adjudicative, and so results in an unsettled appraisal of Jesus since "some" were saying he is a "good man," while others disagreed saying "No, he is deceiving the crowd" (7:12). The talk reflects the expectant crowd's processing of Jesus' identity perhaps due to his absence (7:11), or because of his "secretive" visit to Jerusalem (7:10). Although, at this point, how the characters in the story-world are privy to Jesus' stealth visit is not clear, what is clear is that their collective assessment of him is discordant. Indeed, the entire chapter may be seen as working out whether Jesus is a "good man" or somehow deviant.[2]

---

2. Moloney, *Gospel of John*, 240. That this chapter is principally working out whether Jesus is good or deviant is supported by the fact that the last gossip event of John 7 (vv. 42-52) forms an inclusio with 7:12, as the Pharisees ultimately label Jesus a deviant who has not only led the crowd astray, but the police, too (v. 47).

Leading the crowd astray implies that Jesus' teaching, or Jesus himself, is deceptive (*plannaō*). Since such vocabulary is found in Rabbinic Judaism and associated with the pseudo-Messiah, and eventually works itself out in John 7 with Jesus being associated with a Messianic figure by means of adjudicative gossip,[3] the seriousness of the label is clear in its attempt to undercut Jesus' growing reputation. In any event, although outsiders in this text are divided over whether Jesus is good or deceptive, implying that some outsiders might think him a good man, the reader is not.

The first gossip event in chapter 7 is generated by either Jesus' absence, or his reputation, or both. The rest of the gossip in the chapter is generated by the content of his teaching in the Temple that seems strange to outsiders, and so draws sanctions in the form of aggressive, challenging gossip intended to be overheard publicly and, of course, by Jesus. The narrative moves back and forth between the gossiping and Jesus' responses to the talk in a way that clearly shows how public, third-person, evaluative speech functions as a repetitive challenge to Jesus. In other words, a series of challenges to Jesus' peculiar insider anti-language about his unique relation to the Father, his origins, his destiny, and his invitation to drink, are woven into a long agonistic text describing a rhythmic and relentless discourse (7:25-44):

> Gossip: Now some of the people of Jerusalem were saying, "Is this the man whom they are trying to kill? And here he is, speaking openly, but they say nothing to him! Can it be that the authorities really know that this is the Messiah? Yet we know where this man is from ; but when the Messiah comes, no one will know where he is from." (7:25-27)
>
> Jesus: Then Jesus cried out as he was teaching in the Temple, "You know me, and you know where I am from. I have not come on my own. But the one who sent me is true, and you do not know him. I know him because I am from him, and he sent me." (7:28-29)
>
> Gossip: Yet many in the crowd believed in him and were saying, "When the Messiah comes, will he do more signs than this man has done?" (7:31)

---

3. Ibid., 254-55.

> Jesus: Jesus then said, "I will be with you a little while longer, and then I am going to him who sent me. You will search for me, but you will not find me; and where I am you cannot come." (7:33–34)
>
> Gossip: The Jews said to one another, "Where does this man intend to go that we will not find him? Does he intend to go to the Dispersion among the Greeks and teach the Greeks? What does he mean by saying, 'You will search for me and you will not find me' and 'Where I am, you cannot come'?" (7:35–36)
>
> Jesus: While Jesus was standing there, he cried out, "Let anyone who is thirsty come to me, and let the one who believes in me drink. As the scripture has said, 'Out of the believer's heart shall flow rivers of living water.'" (7:37b–38)
>
> Gossip: When they heard these words, some in the crowd said, "This is really the prophet." Others said, "This is the Messiah." But some asked, "Surely the Messiah does not come from Galilee, does he? Has not the scripture said that the Mesiah is descended from David and comes from Bethlehem, the village where David lived?" So there was a division among them. (7:40–43)

Jesus responds to the challenges, constructing an alternative view of reality than that implied by his opponents. How? The challenges are informed by the Jerusalemites' cultural presumption centered around lineage and education, and affirmed by stereotypical expectations of inhabitants of Galilean villages.[4] Such teaching is not expected of Jesus, the son of a Galilean village artisan (6:42; cf. 1:46). Additionally, the agonistic gossip likely reflects concern over limited good since a village peasant exhibiting such learning is understood to have gained it somehow at another's expense,[5] a notion deflected by Jesus' assertion that the source of his teaching is God (7:16–17).

---

4. Malina and Neyrey, *Portraits of Paul*, 23–24; Moloney, *Gospel of John*, 242.

5. Foster, "Interpersonal Relations," 177, and "Peasant Society," 302.

Constructing a Social Personage

The richness of the gossip in John 7 is remarkable given the intricacy of the exchanges thickly encoded with social values, beliefs, and perspectives on reality. The density of the discourse underscores the important role evaluative talk about persons and events plays in constructing the reality of both events and personages. A number of characteristics, positive and negative, are ascribed to Jesus in the chapter, playing a pivotal role in constituting his identity. Moreover, much of the talk is disputatious (e.g., 7:12, 25-27, 40-43) resulting in dissonant construals of Jesus. In other words, Jesus is the elusive one whose words and deeds are destabilizing enough to render any uniform understanding of him unlikely.

All of the gossip in chapter 7, with the exception of 7:11-12, is generated by the shamanic function of teaching even though only two gossip events *directly* associate Jesus with teaching (7:15, 14). Jesus imparts knowledge a peasant should not possess, thus agonistically goading his auditors to the point that they seek his arrest despite his claims that the new knowledge is not his own (7:16). The new knowledge imparted by his teaching conveys the will of the Father according to which insiders experience reality and live their lives together alternatively to the world of outsiders. In other words, Jesus' in-group, like Jesus himself, walks and talks the new reality envisaged by his teaching that comes from the Father.[6] Additionally, it is on account of his teaching that Jesus is ascribed both positively (7:40) and negatively (7:52b) as a prophetic figure. Again, his peculiar words (7:37b-38) result in his being associated with characters in ancient Israel known at least for speaking their minds if not uttering mysteries about the gift of "living water" (7:38), and so recalling the prophet Moses' gift of water in the wilderness.[7]

Another shamanic feature associated with Jesus in John 7 is the ASC shamanic sky journey that is implied directly by the content of much of the gossip about Jesus' origins.[8] Knowing where Jesus is from (7:27, 41b, 42) and where he is going (7:35-36) are

---

6. Craffert, *Life*, 160-61, 339.
7. Keener, *Gospel of John*, 1:730.
8. Pilch, *Flights of the Soul*.

important thematic concerns for the Evangelist.⁹ Outsiders, of course, either have trouble knowing where Jesus is from, or settle with inadequate knowledge based on earthly categories and often expressed in terms or stereotypes, that is, some of the people of Jerusalem know where Jesus is from (7:27), and the crowd knows he is from Galilee (7:41). Jesus' followers, and hence the reader, know where Jesus is from and where he is going. From the narrative's perspective, knowledge of Jesus' origins is worked out via the literary device of irony.¹⁰ From a cultural perspective, however, discussion of his origins implies knowledge of it, and thus, Jesus' mediation between the human and the Divine as well as his journeys since the beginning (1:1) between the heavenly and earthly realm. This is of course, language of both incarnation (1:14) and resurrection-glorification-ascension (3:13-14; 20:17a). In any event, knowledge of Jesus' origins from the heavens, that is, from God, signals insider understanding of his identity that is contrasted throughout with the misunderstanding of outsiders. This is confirmed by the dichotomy between heavens above and the earth below (spirit/flesh, light/darkness, etc.), and is the backdrop of every discussion about from whom and from where Jesus comes.

The same dichotomy is maintained at John 8:22 where gossip among the Judeans is generated by Jesus' words in the previous verse: "I am going away, and you will search for me, but you will die in your sin. Where I am going, you cannot come" (8:21). The Judeans not surprisingly, misunderstand Jesus' words and so wonder if he is contemplating suicide. Because the judgment on suicide was not uniform in antiquity, the content of the talk could be either positive or negative.¹¹ Either way, what is clear is that they are publicly issuing a challenge.¹² Jesus' response clarifies his origins and so underscores the vast difference between his and theirs, and in familiar terms. Jesus is *anōthen*, that is "from above," and he knows it (8:14, 23; cf. 3:13, 31). He knows as well that he is sent by

---

9. Smith, *John*, 76; Culpepper, *Gospel and Letters of John*, 124-25.
10. See O'Day, *Revelation in the Fourth Gospel*.
11. Keener, *Gospel of John*, 1:743.
12. Ibid., 743; Schnackenburg, *Gospel of John*, 1:198.

the Father who will not leave him (8:27, 29), and he will ultimately return from whence he came.

FROM DARKNESS TO LIGHT: JOHN 9—10:21

Gossip about Jesus is plentiful in the ninth and early tenth chapters of John, and intricately woven into the narrative. A few comments are in order to help bring this section and gossip into clear view. To begin with, the generative event is the healing of the man born blind (John 9:1-7). Although it is not clear if anyone outside of Jesus' disciples actually saw the healing, the narrative commences immediately to describe in some detail how the event is received by several characters in their attempt to make sense of, or better, (re)construct reality which has been unsettled by the healing. Talk commences among "the neighbors" (9:8-12), the Pharisees and the man born blind (9:13-17), the parents of the blind man and the Judeans (9:18-23), the man born blind and the Judeans (9:24-34), and finally, among the Judeans (10:19-21). The subject of each of the gossip events alternates from the man born blind to Jesus two times in the narrative (man born blind, 9:8-12, 18-23; Jesus, 9:13-17, 24-34; 10:19-21). Most conspicuous about all of the gossip is that it is adjudicative, that is, those engaged in the discourse are either in explicit disagreement over how to appraise the subject (Jesus), or they are unsuccessful in making sense of the events about which they talk. It will be suggested below that, ultimately, Jesus is the subject of all of the gossip in John 9—10:21.

The Healing of the Man Born Blind

As mentioned earlier, the generative event of the gossip in John 9 is the restoration of sight to a man "blind from birth" (9:1) by Jesus, who is walking along with his disciples when he comes across the blind man. The ensuing discussion between Jesus and his disciples is crucial for the story as it sets up dual categories for understanding the source of the blindness. How one understands the source of the man's blindness reflects where one stands vis-à-vis Jesus. The conventional, "earthly" notion (see 3:12!) sees the man's blindness as a result of sin—either his sin, or his parents' sin (9:2)—in congruence with the notion of deeds and consequences. In much Israelite literature, blindness is understood to be the result of either individual sin, or collective sin (Exod 20:5; *1 Enoch* 98.5), and would also have social effects such as separation from, or loss of one's place in one's community. From the start, the disciples understand the blindness in terms of "deeds and consequences" since they ask Jesus whether it was the blind man's sin, or his parents' sin that caused the blindness (9:2). This suggests some misunderstanding on the disciples' part, and is likely a recollection of shaky insider standing among those who are Jesus' followers (see 6:60). Jesus' reply circumvents deeds and consequences altogether by contextualizing the healing in his self-identifying claim to be the light of the world (9:5b) and thus, begins the blind man's step-by-step initiation into Jesus' group.

The healing of the man born blind unhinges the order and routine of the constructed world of the neighbors first, then the Pharisees, then the Judeans, and so gives rise to subsequent attempts to (re)construct reality in acceptable terms in a string of gossip events.[13] As will become evident, all of the talk is critical or evaluative, and in some way, adjudicative in character. The resulting dissonant assessments of Jesus are crucial to the eventual working out of Jesus' identity in the Fourth Gospel.

Gossip About the Man Born Blind, I: The Neighbors

The neighbors try to put their world back in order in light of the healing event first by gossiping, in third person speech, about the man's identity, whether or not he is the man who "used to sit and beg" (9:8). Their gossip is adjudicative as they are divided with "some" (*alloi*) saying it is him, and "others" (*alloi*) saying "No, but it is someone like him" (9:a). This gossip event, deliberating the formerly blind man's identity, anticipates the same deliberation soon to follow over Jesus' identity. Indeed, the interrogation of the man

---

13. Botha, "Social Dynamics," 211–12.

can be seen as an interrogation of the conspicuously absent Jesus as at least two parallels can be drawn between the man born blind and Jesus in this first scenario following the healing. First, the neighbors are divided over the formerly blind man's identity, as are many throughout John's gospel over Jesus' identity (cf. 3:17; 7:12). Second, Jesus, the one sent from God, directs the formerly blind man to wash at Siloam "which means Sent" (9:7a).[14] The man's response to the neighbors "I am (he)" (*egō eimi*) (9:9b; cf. 8:58), reflects Jesus' absolute "I am" sayings throughout the gospel (4:26; 6:20, 35, 41, 48, 51; 8:12, 18, 23 (twice), 24, 28, 58; 10:7, 9, 11, 14; 11:25; 13:19; 14:6; 15:1, 5; 18:5, 6, 8). Such parallels imply what is made explicit by the neighbors' direct interrogation of the man, that is, that Jesus, despite his absence, is clearly the subject of all of the gossip in this chapter. In any event, the adjudicative gossip at 9:8-9 and the subsequent responses by the man born blind, yield little precision as to Jesus' identity among the discussants since no one appears to know where Jesus is (9:12), and not knowing something about Jesus, in this gospel, is significant.

Gossip About Jesus, I: The Pharisees and the Man Born Blind

After vigorously defending his identity to the neighbors, the man born blind is then brought by the neighbors to the Pharisees to see if they can help make sense of the unnerving event that has occurred (9:13-17). Interestingly, although the neighbors were initially interested in the man's identity and eventually, how the event occurred in the first place, the Pharisees interrogation elides into gossip as the man born blind again (see 9:11) describes the details of what Jesus actually did (9:15). "Some" (*tines*) of the Pharisees gossip negatively about Jesus with respect to his origins: "This man is not from God, for he does not observe the Sabbath" (9:16a). The confidence displayed by the Pharisees' knowledge about Jesus' origins is

---

14. Fifty-one times in John's gospel Jesus is said to be "sent" from the Father. Malina and Rohrbaugh, *Social-Science Commentary on the Gospel of John*, 170.

Gossiping Jesus

conspicuous as it evades the actually healing itself.[15] However, not all are so confident, so "others" (*alloi*) among the Pharisees undercut the initial gossip noting how incongruous it is that a "sinner," that is, someone who doesn't keep the Sabbath, is able to heal a man born blind (9:16b); such a man may after all, be from God. Thus, the Pharisees' attempt to construct Jesus in light of the healing of the man born blind, results in a dissonant construal that is explicitly stated by the narrator (9:16b). On the one hand, Jesus' "signs" imply positively that he is not a sinner (*hamartōlos*), and so, contrary to "some" of the Pharisees, that he is from God (cf. 3:9). On the other hand, since he does not keep the Sabbath, he is not from God, and therefore, a sinner (9:24). This negative gossip construes the subject in typical terms concerned with origins, and by means of deviance labeling, attempts to encode Jesus' identity negatively given the out of place nature of the healing of a man born blind presumably because of sin.

The Pharisees' dilemma is acute and should not be overlooked seeing that the healing of the blind man has unhinged their understanding of the proper religious order of things.[16] On the one hand, Jesus healed a man "blind from birth" (9:1) which for the Pharisees, clearly indicates the sinfulness of the man (9:2, 34; cf. Ezek 18:20; Ps 89:33). On the other hand, Jesus was able to heal, as far as this group of Pharisees is concerned, by breaking the Sabbath (mixing a muddy balm) even though God "does not listen to sinners" (9:31; cf. Isa 1:15; Pss 66:18; 109:7; 145:19; Prov 15:8, 29; Job 27:9; 35:13). In the face of their religious world turned upside down, it is understandable that the Pharisees' gossip is argumentative. The result of their dissonance over Jesus' origins, and whether or not he is a sinner thus, results in schism that is explicitly stated (*kai schisma ēn en autois*; 9:16b).

A number of paradigmatic outsiders relative to Jesus' in-group are portrayed as coming close to construing Jesus from an insider's standpoint, imagining that Jesus may be from God due to the signs he performs. The adjudicative nature of the gossip lucidly displays

15. Keener, *Gospel of John*, 1:786.
16. O'Day, *Word Disclosed*, 77–83.

the constructive vitality of this mode of speech, as well as the potential for a wide range of opinion that often accompanies such talk, and may result in schism. The division among the Pharisees has the further outcome of inviting the formerly blind man in on the discourse, and who provisionally suggests Jesus is a prophet (9:17; cf. 7:40). Thus, taken in its entirety, the construal of Jesus comprises a number of elements toward constituting his identity, but without offering a clear, unified portrait. The outsiders who do not know Jesus are divided over how to construe him in light of the healing; some focus on their own notion of Sabbath violation, thus ignoring the sign itself, while others focus on the sign and move closer to an insider's perspective. The stumbling of the "others" toward insider knowledge stands in contrast to the man born blind who is clearly moving closer to understanding who Jesus is, beginning first from the position of an outsider (9:12). The epistemological crisis regarding Jesus' identity is the catalyst here, as it is for the entire Fourth Gospel, and is plainly illustrated at this point as the objective goal of the gossip. The knowledge about Jesus' identity is conveyed by Jesus' signs that reveal him (2:11; 3:2), and by the knowledge he imparts by his teaching (7:46). Presumably Jesus knows who he is, at least as far as he is construed by his primary group. And although outsiders either do not know him, or construct him inadequately (7:27-29, 49, 51; 8:14, 27-28, 32, 43, 52, 55), the potential for insider misunderstanding is not unprecedented (6:60, 66). While this crisis is not somewhat relieved until John 10,[17] it is brought to the fore again here as it was in chapter 6, and portrayed as a crisis capable of unsettling group unity. In any event, it is worth recognizing that the key functional element of the working out of the crisis is speech and talk.

---

17. Whether or not it is relieved at all by the end of John's gospel is, I think, an open question. Settling on any construal of Jesus is consistently shown to be inadequate in this gospel.

Gossip About the Man Born Blind, II: The Judeans and the Parents

While it is conspicuous that the "Judeans" rather than the Pharisees now call on the parents of the man born blind, it is probable that the Evangelist is simply toggling between the two indiscriminately.[18] The text at this point is not clear if the man born blind is present or not. Given that 9:24 says the man had to be called "for the second time," it is likely he was not present to overhear the interrogative gossip between his parents and the Judeans.

Turning away from the healing itself, the Judeans seek to discredit the condition of the man in the first place; was he blind from birth, let alone even blind at all, or not? The disbelief behind the Judeans' inquiry about whether the man had been blind form birth, and thus whether a healing took place or not, is in striking contrast to the previous scene when the Pharisees (but here, the Judeans) invited the man into their gossip to offer his construal of Jesus in light of their division over his identity. There, they affirmed that his eyes were opened by Jesus (9:17), while here (9:18) they are in disbelief that the man was born blind at all, let alone "miraculously" healed.

The parents declare that the man is their son, and that he was born blind and so, positively assess him and the validity of the miracle (9:20) despite the line of interrogation by the Pharisees. The information they offer at first, is relatively safe. But when considering how their son came to see, and who it was that "opened his eyes," they are more cautious given the potential consequences for speaking about Jesus openly—expulsion from the Synagogue (9:21–23).[19] The seriousness of expulsion from the Synagogue is a considerable threat since the separation from a group vital to one's self-identity and livelihood often had dire consequences in the ancient world. Moreover, since it is likely the parents were impoverished (allowing their son to beg; 9:8), for them to be found unattached to the group was an intolerable fate to be avoided.[20] Thus, the parents shift

---

18. Barrett, *Gospel According to St. John*, 360.

19. Carson, *Gospel*, 369.

20. Keener, *Gospel of John*, 1:787; Malina and Rohrbaugh, *Social-Science Commentary on the Gospel of John*, 112

the onus back onto their son since "he is of age" and will speak for himself (9:21).

Gossip About Jesus, II: The Judeans and the Man Born Blind

Eventually, the desperate situation of the Pharisees (or Judeans) brought on by the healing is exacerbated when the formerly blind man uses their own logic to underscore how dislodged their religious worldview has become in light of what has happened (9:24–34). This gossip event is peculiarly tensive since it involves the transaction and control of information about the still absent Jesus' character (since 9:7), his ability to heal, his leadership, and his origins.

The talk is initiated by the Judeans who again draw the man into the evaluative discourse, this time charging him to take an oath, "Give Glory to God!" and then labeling Jesus a "sinner" (9:24). In light of Jesus' healing the man born blind, which has upturned the Judeans' understanding of how God is operative in the world, they assert what they think they know about Jesus' origins, identity, and character in an attempt to control the ensuing information transaction, that is, to (re)construct the world in a way that makes sense of what has occurred. In order to make sense of it, and thus, to maintain the status quo that existed before the healing even occurred, the Judeans need to conduct an information exchange that successfully discredits the healing somehow, and so dishonors Jesus. This partially explains the deviance accusation of 9:24 emphatically voiced as knowledge: "We know this man is a sinner." Their attempt to control the information, and so the construction of Jesus, does not go unchallenged as the formerly blind man, unlike the Judeans, first responds asserting what he does not know (9:25a; cf. v. 12b), followed by what he knows, that is, that a healing has indeed, taken place (9:25b). The Judeans' demand that the man relate again how Jesus healed him suggests their world remains unhinged (9:26). Responding that he has already told them the story, the man asks two incisive questions: "Why do you want to hear it again? Do you also want to become his disciples?" (9:27). This likely does not reflect a naïve hope that the Judeans may actually seek to become

95

Jesus' disciples although hearing stories of Jesus' signs is part of the process of becoming one.[21] Instead, the man's second question is preceded by a negative particle in the Greek indicating that he expects a negative answer, and thus, should be seen as a counter-challenge to the Judeans. The Judeans counter emphatically that the man born blind is "his (Jesus') disciple," that they are disciples of Moses (to whom God has spoken), and that they know nothing of Jesus' origins (9:28-29). The Judeans' claim to be disciples of Moses draws out their in-group identity over-against Jesus and his group. Moreover, their claim is in terms of their knowledge of Moses' mediatory relationship with God who has spoken through him, and ironically highlights Jesus' superior role even more.

The man responds by using the same principles evinced by the Pharisees to disparage Jesus (9:16, 24; 9:2!), thus making a case for Jesus' origins from God (9:30-33). In other words, the man born blind takes on a teaching role in this gossip event (9:34), by imparting knowledge about Jesus' origins and identity in the face of the challenge leveled by the Judeans in their gossip. This is another example of how the story draws a parallel between Jesus and the man born blind who not only functions as an advocate for the absent Jesus, but directly represents Jesus in his absence as the subject of all the gossip in the chapter. Like Jesus, the man is sent (9:7), is "I am" (*egō eimi*, 9:9b), and teaches (9:30-33). In other words, throughout John 9, Jesus is the actual subject of the gossip, even when the man born blind is the apparent subject.

The Judeans' response to the man's teaching is to cast him out of the synagogue, which in Jesus' culture is a tacit admission they have lost the verbal dispute with the man over Jesus' identity. This element of the challenge-riposte characterizes much of the exchange of information in the gossip event, suggesting that when gossip involves the transactional concern for controlling information about the subject it may take on peculiarly agonistic features. After all, Jesus' identity and reputation are under construction in this text, as is the formerly blind man's.

---

21. Keener, *Gospel of John*, 1:790; Moloney, *Gospel of John*, 294.

Gossip About Jesus, III: The Judeans Divided Over the Shepherd

Eventually, the man born blind, who has served as the surrogate subject of gossip about Jesus and participated in gossiping about him, is brought fully into Jesus' group (9:35–38). His new knowledge and standing as a member of Jesus' group stands in stark relief to the knowledge and standing of the Pharisees (Judeans) with whom sin abides (9:41). Indeed, their confident claim to knowledge is contrasted with the humility of the man born blind (9:12b) who, unlike the Pharisees/Judeans, is open to receiving revelation. Ironically, the Pharisees'/Judeans' knowledge is disclosed as that which keeps them in the very situation they consistently construe Jesus as being in, that is, abiding with sin (9:41; cf. vv. 16, 24).

Jesus' declaration that sin abides with the Judeans because of their self-confident knowledge is the beginning of a long discourse (10:1–18), the meaning of which escapes the Judeans. In it, Jesus' anti-language describes the character of the relationship between group members, his relationship to them, and his role as leader of the group. Jesus is the "sheep gate" (*hē thura tōn probatōn*), the entryway into the group (10:7). Jesus is the "good shepherd" (*ho poimēn ho kalos*), the leader of the group protecting the flock from wolves (10:11; cf. vv. 1–5). As the "sheep gate" Jesus functions as broker between the Divine patron in the heavens and his clients, the disciples. Neyrey describes the shepherd as one sent by God to "mediate knowledge, power, loyalty, and material benefaction" from God, and to broker their interests by prayer.[22] Jesus as the "good shepherd" situates his identity deeply within the cultural world of honor-shame since the adjective "good" (*kalos*) can be understood as the opposite of "shame" (*aischros*) rather than "evil" (*ponēros*). Calling himself the "good" or "noble" shepherd, Jesus unites his identity with the notion of a "noble death" (10:11) that was part of the rhetoric of encomia in the ancient Hellenistic world.[23] Thus, both labels used by Jesus are operative within his social-cultural world and imply information about his relationship with both

---

22. Neyrey, "I Am the Door," 272.
23. Neyrey, "Nobel Shepherd," 268.

his Father and his followers. The labels then, serve to highlight boundaries, and to affirm identity and loyalty among the group and its leader by describing the contours of a dyadic relationship between Jesus (the shepherd) and the Father (10:15), the shepherd and the sheep (10:14), and among the sheep (10:16).[24]

The reception of the man born blind into Jesus' faction (9:1-41) is followed by a section describing relational dynamics of the faction in language reflecting the agonistic honor-shame culture of ancient Palestine wherein group membership, identity, and loyalty were paramount. Jesus' discourse on the sheep, shepherd, and sheep gate is the generative event for the Judeans' gossip (10:19-21) that is, again, disputatious as discussants come to alternative understandings of Jesus. Recalling similar gossip events (7:12, 25-27, 46-48; 9:8-9, 16, 24-34), Jesus is on the one hand labeled deviant by demon possession (10:20), while on the other hand the healing of the blind man, and Jesus' power to heal, are affirmed (10:21). Once again, the Evangelist does not relieve the tension as Jesus' identity is continually under construction.

Gossiping the Raising of Lazarus: John 11:1-57

Since John 5:18 the tension between Jesus and his opponents has been on the increase with many deciding that Jesus should be arrested or killed (5:18; 7:30, 32; 8:59; 10:31, 39). Although most of Jesus' opponents are portrayed as operating against him, some outsiders have been described either coming to some sort of faith in him, or at least, cautious in their construal of him—an element emphasized in many of the adjudicative gossip events (7:12, 25-27, 31, 46; 8:30; 9:16b; 10:21).

The story of the raising of Lazarus functions as the climax of the other signs Jesus performs although following bitter conflict.[25] As the climax of Jesus' signs, it is peculiar since it follows a different pattern than the others. Previous signs are first described, and then

---

24. Malina and Rohrbaugh, *Social-Science Commentary on the Gospel of John*, 179-81.
25. Schnackenburg, *Gospel of John*, 2:325.

followed by interpretive discourse making sense of the sign. In John 11, the sign (vv. 43–44) is preceded by three conversations involving Jesus—with the disciples (11:7–6), with Martha (11:17–27), and with Mary (11:28–34)—that interpret the sign before it happens.[26] The key text for understanding the theological significance of the sign comes as Jesus exclaims, "I am the resurrection and the life. Those who believe in me, even though they die, will live" (11:25). Moreover, an inclusio is formed around the story, framed on one side by Jesus' words relating what is soon to occur is to glorify God (11:4), and on the other by the prophetic utterance of Caiaphas (11:49–50) concerning Jesus' impending death.[27] In other words, the inclusio indicates that the Son will be glorified through the resurrection of Lazarus, not because of the sign itself, but because it will eventually lead to Jesus' death by crucifixion which is in John's gospel, Jesus' glorification (3:14!).

Although the presence of a lively gossip network is implied a number of times in the story (11:3–4, 20, 28–29, 46), there are only three gossip events described in any detail, all three inferring an agonistic context of honor-shame and reputation (11:36–37, 46–37, 56). A face-to-face event occurs immediately after the third interpretive conversation between Jesus and Mary (11:28–34). The gossip emerges amongst the Judeans, generated by Jesus' weeping, presumably because of Lazarus's death (11:35). The gossip is adjudicative since the information that Jesus loved Lazarus (11:36) is immediately undercut by "some" (*tines*) of the Judeans who raise an interesting question: "So the Judeans said, 'See how he loved him!' But some of them said, 'Could not he who opened the eyes of the blind man have kept this man from dying?'" (11:36–37). The text suggests the gossip network has carried the news about Jesus' healing the man born blind. The negative adverb at 11:37 (*ouk*) signals that some Judeans expect Jesus to be able to raise Lazarus, thus the gossip at this point expresses their frustration over his absence. This accounts for the negative appraisal, leveled in response to Jesus' display of love for Lazarus, targeting Jesus' "dynamic dawdling" upon

---

26. Culpepper, *Gospel and Letters of John*, 185.
27. Moloney, *Gospel of John*, 325.

Gossiping Jesus

hearing the news of his sick friend (11:6; 2:4; 4:48; 7:6–9),[28] and not targeting his reputation as a healer since he fails to save Lazarus because of his delayed arrival.[29] The adjudicative gossip attempts to construe Jesus' display of mourning in two distinctly different ways. Most of the Judeans present see Jesus mourning the death of one of his kin, like the other Judeans present (11:32–33). But "some" of them see Jesus as rather indifferent toward his friend (11:11; cf. 15:14), thus calling into question his group loyalty.[30] Both constructions of Jesus miss the mark however, since Jesus' weeping at 11:35 (*dakruō*) is not like the "crying" (*klaiō*) of the rest of the Judeans present (11:32–33), since he is likely expressing sadness over Mary's earthly understanding of events she shares with the Judeans.[31]

Upon raising Lazarus from the dead, the narrative reports that while many of the Judeans believed in Jesus (11:45), "some of them" (*tines de ex autōn*) informed the Pharisees about what Jesus had done (11:46) resulting in a meeting of the council (*sunedrion*) that quickly evolves into a gossip event (11:47–50). Articulating concerns over their own loss of reputation in light of Jesus' burgeoning popularity, the council imagines the eventual Roman reaction toward the Temple and "our nation" to be a violent one (11:47). What is clear is that the raising of Lazarus is not the generative cause of the gossip, since the sign was not the source of Jesus' impending glorification. Rather, the cause of the gossip is the concern that many of the Judeans who witnessed the raising of Lazarus now believed in Jesus because of it (11:45). Such belief (*pisteuō*) signals the addition of new members into Jesus' in-group, and so instigates the concern over his growing reputation, and that of his faction.[32]

---

28. Malina and Rohrbaugh, *Social-Science Commentary on the Gospel of John*, 68, 193.

29. Moloney, *Gospel of John*, 331.

30. Malina and Rohrbaugh, *Social-Science Commentary on the Gospel of John*, 68, 197.

31. Moloney, *Gospel of John*, 331.

32. Malina and Rohrbaugh, *Social-Science Commentary on the Gospel of John*, 202.

This gossip event may as well, be seen within the context of what Neyrey calls the "sociology of secrecy" since it involves information control and the dissemination of knowledge via espionage.[33] Thus, the narrative indicates that the spies of the elite group who witnessed the raising of Lazarus and the resulting growth of Jesus' popularity, report the disconcerting information to the Pharisees and the Chief Priests (cf. 5:15). The reaction of the council reflects the first-century Mediterranean social concern over "limited good," thus, suggesting that Jesus' growth in reputation comes at their expense. Injured by Jesus' success, the council engages in envy which, when directed at Jesus, turns into violence plotted according to Caiaphas's design with the aim of shaming Jesus, scattering his followers, and restoring the council's honor.[34]

Gossiping a Shamanic Figure

The components of the gossip events in John 11 that most directly imply the shamanic complex are healing combined with the idea of a holy man's heavenly journey. In the first-century Mediterranean worldview, it was granted that non-human and/or divine beings influenced many aspects of human life so that sickness was understood to be directly caused by a particular agent, that is, a spirit or a demon. Moreover, within the first-century shamanic worldview, shamanic figures—"holy men"—were known to travel to other realms in behalf of the sick in order to "rescue" them from the malady.[35] The "raising of Lazarus" can thus be seen within the framework of such healing along with other texts describing Jesus "raising" other persons (Mark 5:35–43; Luke 7:1–17).[36] Jesus, the shamanic figure who controls nature and the elements (John 2:9; 6:11, 19), and heals (John 5:8–9; 9:1–6), travels to other known realms to execute the healing.

---

33. Neyrey, *Gospel of John*, 205–6.
34. Ibid.
35. Craffert, *Life*, 159, 181–82, 185.
36. Malina and Rohrbaugh, *Social-Science Commentary on the Synoptic Gospels*, 168, 253.

6

Conclusions

GOSSIPING A GALILEAN SHAMAN

PIETER CRAFFERT'S BOOK *Life of a Galilean Shaman* stands as a serious reconsideration of the focus of historical Jesus research in a direction that more sufficiently addresses the sociological and anthropological elements of the canonical Gospels' cumulative portrait of Jesus. As an exercise in "anthropological historiography," the book fills in a number of gaps left open by the "reigning paradigm," and thus offers the conversation tools useful for a more culturally plausible historical Jesus.

This project sought to utilize the methodological matrix of the shamanic complex appropriated by Craffert as part of a social-scientific framework for seeing the text of John's gospel through the lens of gossip in order to determine how such talk colludes with various social values and processes to construct Jesus' identity. The elements of the framework, or "model," included a working definition of gossip and the shamanic complex, as well as a procedure for moving between the text and the model called "abduction," that both made sense of what was being looked at in the text, and continually adjusted the framework itself as the text disclosed aspects of gossip and its role in constituting Jesus' identity in John.[1]

1. See "Living with Models," in chapter 1 above.

Gossiping Jesus

Although this project clearly suggests the "sort of man" that occasions the gossip in John's gospel is a shamanic figure, the shamanic complex is not a requisite element for the gossip model to successfully "facilitate understanding" about Jesus and the processes involved in constituting him as a social personage.

Gossip was seen to be face-to-face evaluative talk, between persons or among a group, about a third-party subject who is either actually absent, or rendered absent to the conversation. Moreover, gossip was observed emerging in response to a "generative event"—words and deeds that challenge or undermine the *status quo* and/or the expected social script—in a sense-making attempt to (re)assert or (re)construct social reality. The character and content of the talk was then viewed through the shamanic complex, that is, a "homomorphic" constellation of various features and functions associated with the cross-cultural social type of a shaman. The features associated with a shamanic figure, and thus comprising the shamanic complex include ASCs, spirit possession, and heavenly "sky" journeys while various social functions include healing, divination, control of animals and spirits, prophecy, and teaching—all of which were seen to be associated with gossip about Jesus in John. All elements of the framework were taken into consideration, and utilized to see the Fourth Gospel differently, and with remarkable results. As highlighted throughout the project, Jesus is linked via gossip to ASC experiences (1:32–34), heavenly journeys (1:29, 36; 6:42; 9:16, 33; 11:45, 47; 12:29; 16:17–18),[2] and spirit possession (1:32–34; 10:20). Moreover, he is linked to several social functions such as healing, control of animals and nature (3:2; 5:11; 6:14; 7:31; 9:8–34; 10:21; 11:45, 47), prophecy (1:48–49; 4:17–19; 9:17), ritual (1:32–34; 3:26), and teaching (3:2; 6:52; 7:15). The gossip about Jesus in John's gospel associates, or directly connects Jesus with the various features and functions of the shamanic complex, and so, plausibly ascribes the Johannine Jesus as a shamanic figure.

Although linking textual reports of an oral phenomenon to a cross-cultural social type was an important aspect of the project,

---

2. Although not dealt with in detail above, both gossip events at 12:29 and 16:17–18 imply Jesus' origins from the heavens, and the shamanic feature of ASC induced sky journeys.

Conclusions

this was not the primary aim. The primary aim was to see how gossip is operative in John's story-world, along with other social processes and values of the ancient Mediterranean world, in constituting Jesus' social identity. To begin with, the content of much of the gossip about Jesus is indeterminate, that is, the gossipers cannot come to an unambiguous conclusion about who or what Jesus is. This sort of gossip, dubbed "adjudicative gossip" (e.g., 7:25–27; 9:16; 10:19–21), is likely intended to forecast the Evangelist's intent to portray Jesus as one whose identity is ultimately inscrutable, to both insiders and outsiders, and thus, always "under construction." Indeed, not holding on to who or what one thinks Jesus is (20:17!), and always beginning such an enquiry with humility (9:12) is something fleshed out in John's narrative by means of indeterminate, adjudicate discourse. Jesus is socially constructed by the talk as a rather ambiguous figure: good, bad, deceptive, not a sinner, a sinner, from Nazareth, from above, son of Joseph, son of the Father, teacher, prophet, demon possessed, filled with the Holy Spirit, etc. This construction stands in apparent contrast to the Johannine prologue establishing Jesus as the Logos who was with God in the beginning, and is God (1:1–18). However, followed as that is by a flurry of titular honoring by several characters (1:19–49), it is clear that who Jesus is (the Logos) is apparently received variously by human beings whose experience of him yields a rather complex character, and thus, suggests the importance if not the necessity of the ongoing construction of Jesus. To be sure, Jesus is certainly not one to be held on to.

Gossip was also seen to be intricately operative in the ascription and distribution of honor and shame through the agonistic social process of challenge-riposte. On a number of occasions, gossip is uttered with the intent of being overheard by the subject so that it functions simultaneously as a public challenge, as well as a public construal of Jesus' identity. Interestingly, challenges rendered in the form of gossip are made at the risk of losing control of the information transaction since the one(s) issuing such a challenge is basically inviting others—the "public court of reputation"[3]—to engage

---

3. Crook, "Honor, Shame, and Social Status Revisited."

in the construal of the subject by means of their discourse. In any event, in such gossip events one can see the eliding of social process and pivotal value—gossip and the transaction of honor. Although it is true that such gossip events constituting challenges over honor are particularly aggressive, they clearly embody the collusion of social processes and values with the construction of social reality and identity.

Christology "From the Side" and the Historical Jesus

Looking at Jesus' identity through the lens of gossip provides a Christological glimpse of Jesus "from the side."[4] This is different than the high Christology "from above" or the low Christology "from below" focusing as they do on titles applied to Jesus and his human, usually the physical (thirst, exhaustion, etc.) or emotional (anger, empathy, sadness, etc.) characteristics of the "word made *flesh*." More nuanced than that, this project viewed the enfleshed Word of John's gospel, as one thoroughly embedded in the socio-cultural world of the first-century Mediterranean. This angle provides the backdrop for seeing how persons, both insiders and outsiders, are remembered to have first experienced Jesus' words and deeds (generative events) and initiated processes of sense making, as well as reality and identity construction, by means of the social process of gossip. This is not intended to imply a claim for or against the narratives describing gossip as eyewitness, verbatim accounts of the social process—or, as the reigning paradigm might put it, "historical reportage." It is rather, a claim to the socio-cultural embeddedness of the first followers and subsequent communities that emerged in light of the words and deeds of an extraordinary historical figure. Put another way, this project is "historical" in terms of the degree to which it has sought to see cultural stories about cultural events described in the Fourth Gospel, and particularly by connecting literary features of oral phenomena (gossip) to the life of a social personage thoroughly immersed in

4. Malina and Neyrey, *Calling Jesus Names*.

Conclusions

his world.[5] What has been suggested is the cultural plausibility of such events since the narrative reflects the social and cultural reality from which it emerged. Subsequently, the extent to which the gossip in John adheres to the methodology and evinces a shamanic figure, suggests the historical and cultural plausibility of both the events themselves, and the words and deeds of the historical figure that catalyzed such discourse. In other words, the sort of man that generated the gossip was a shamanic figure. Thus, gossip renders a plausible portrait of how such a figure may have been experienced in his socio-cultural milieu. Although the gossip in John may indeed function the way a chorus did in ancient Greco-Roman dramas,[6] which would imply the talk was simply "made up" by the author, it is just as possible that material judged "authentic" by the reigning historical Jesus paradigm was made up too, since, like this project, the material's adhesion to criteria constructed by that methodology itself determines "historicity."[7]

Gossiping Jesus in Communities of Faithful Discourse

The talk about Jesus in John is both fascinating and compelling. Gossip about him is not meaningless talk ("chatter") or obfuscated "spin" barely approaching some truth. Certainly, for those who experienced his words and deeds, gossip was a powerful force for piecing together what Jesus said and did, and thus, gave form and substance to his words and deeds, and to his social identity.

By paying attention to the gossip about Jesus, the reader is gifted with a look at how important social discourse, both positive and negative in character, is in constituting his identity. Indeed,

---

5. I am using the word "historical" to describe the gossip events in John insofar as the meaning and occurrence of the social process is construed using the methodology appropriated throughout, namely, a social-scientific model of gossip. In other words, this is a subjective, intentional *construction* of the past, not "the past" itself. See Martin, *Pedagogy of the Bible*, 40–44.

6. Brant, *Dialogue and Drama*, 178–87.

7. Craffert, *Life*, 96–99; Daniels, "Gossip in John's Gospel," 25–26.

Gossiping Jesus

Christian communities of faith can learn from this gospel the importance of intentionality in faithful discourse that construes not only who Jesus is, but the community's identity as well.[8] Particular contexts of discourse in faithful communities include, among others, informal social/fellowship, religious education, evangelistic, liturgical, ritual, and homiletic. While much of the talk in these contexts is understandably scripted to convey positive appraisal of Jesus and God, John's gospel suggests the importance of hosting both positive and even ambiguous evaluation of Jesus since settling too easily on any one particular construction of him, runs the risk of closing a community off from experiencing him in fresh new ways.[9]

John's gospel is not the only place in the Bible where one can find such hosting of ambiguous appraisal of the Divine. Israel's "murmuring" about God in the wilderness, the protestations of the lament psalms, as well as the books of Lamentations and Job, all model a faithful community's honest appraisal and complex construal of God. The murmuring about Jesus in John's gospel is similarly ambiguous in its portrait of one who is inscrutable and enlightening, compassionate and uncompromising, confrontational and kind, secretive and direct. A character of such complexity

---

8. Groups often embody their identity in a prototypical, ideal figure from the past. See Baker, "Social Identity Theory," 132. Thus, Christians identify Jesus as such a figure who, through processes of social memory, functions as the model of thinking and behavior for believers who identify themselves as being "in Christ." Indeed, for early believers in Jesus, the use of stereotypical self-referents became an important element of identity construction and maintenance, and is thus reflected in the Pauline epistles where believers are "in Christ" (e.g., Rom 8:1; 12:5), conformed to "the image of his Son" (Rom 8:29), or even "conformed to his death" (Phil 3:10). See Esler, *Galatians*, 40–57. Such intra-group stereotyping was a vital part of the processes of social memory that both called forth the early believers' memory of their savior, but also provided key facets of their collective self-identity.

9. See O'Day, *Word Disclosed*, 63–90. The fact that much "God/Jesus talk" in contexts of faith is "scripted" positively raises several interesting questions: Is such positive appraisal only scripted, or is it sometimes coerced? What difference does the character of the context make? Are formal settings always more controlled than informal settings? See Bailey, "Informal Controlled Oral Tradition."

Conclusions

is bound to elicit a diversity of experiences. This begs interesting questions: What of the Pharisees' experience of being shamed by Jesus when he turns his back to them, and engages the crowd in contemptuous gossip about them (Matt 22:41—23:36)? What of Peter's and the other eleven disciples' experience, when both their choice to remain with him and their collective recognition that he is the "Holy One of God," are ignored by Jesus who instead focuses on the impending betrayal (John 6:70)? What of the Syro-Phoenician woman's experience of Jesus insulting her and her child by calling them "dogs" (Mark 7:27)? She sought out Jesus because of the gossip network's positive construal of him as a healer and a holy man (Mark 7:24), but was only able to gain a favorable result after countering his insult with a clever response (Mark 7:28).[10] Together, these and other similar scenarios underscore the fact that Jesus, both within and without the text, was experienced in ways provocative and unsettling enough to generate vigorous discourse in the form of gossip. Perhaps these and similarly ambiguous snapshots of Jesus did not constitute the target believers, seeking to be "conformed to the image of his Son" (Rom 8:29), were aiming at. Nevertheless, they were, and still are poignantly unvarnished memories of Jesus, commemorated orally and textually by faithful communities, and thus are constitutive elements of their collective identity as followers of Christ.

The complexity of Jesus' identity is, in large part, due to the various ways he was, and still is experienced by people—insiders and outsiders, Christians and non-Christians. Although, the Gospels ultimately seek to portray Jesus in a positive light, it is not an unambiguous portrait. This is attested by the variety of mundane encounters with Jesus generating gossip that would eventually coalesce to fund the traditioning process, and is there to be seen in the text if one looks for it. This is something worth learning from the endlessly adjudicative gossip about Jesus in John—"endlessly" adjudicative since *who* the one "from above" *is*, let alone who he *was*, is endlessly under construction.

---

10. Malina and Rohrbaugh, *Social-Science Commentary on the Synoptic Gospels*, 177.

Bibliography

Alexander, Loveday. "The Living Voice: Skepticism Towards the Written Word in Early Christian and Graeco-Roman Texts." In *The Bible in Three Dimensions: Essays in Celebration of Forty Years of Biblical Studies in the University of Sheffield*, edited by David J. A. Clines, Stephen E. Fowl, and Stanley E. Porter, 221-48. Sheffield: JSOT, 1990.

Aristotle. *Aristotle: Nicomachean Ethics*. Translated and edited by Roger Crisp. Cambridge: Cambridge University Press, 2004.

———. *The Religion of Paul the Apostle*. New Haven: Yale University Press, 2000.

Ashton, John. *Understanding the Fourth Gospel*. Oxford: Clarendon, 1991.

Bailey, Kenneth E. "Informal Controlled Oral Tradition and the Synoptic Gospels." *Themelios* 20 (1995) 4-11.

Baker, Coleman A. "Social Identity Theory and Biblical Interpretation." *Biblical Theology Bulletin* 42 (2012) 129-38.

Barrett, Charles K. *The Gospel According to St. John: An Introduction with Commentary and Notes on the Greek Text*. Philadelphia: Westminster, 1978.

Batten, Alicia. "Brokerage: Jesus as Social Entrepreneur." In *Understanding the Social World of the New Testament*, edited by Dietmar Neufeld and Richard E. DeMaris, 167-77. New York: Routledge, 2010.

———. "The Patron-Client Institution: God in the Letter of James: Patron or Benefactor." In *The Social World of the New Testament*, edited by Jerome H. Neyrey and Eric C. Stewart, 47-61. Grand Rapids: Baker, 2008.

Bergmann, Jorg R. *Discreet Indiscretions: The Social Organization of Gossip*. New York: Aldine de Gruyter, 1993.

Botha, Pieter J. J. "Paul and Gossip: A Social Mechanism in Early Christian Communities." *Neotestamentica* 32 (1998) 267-88.

———. "The Social Dynamics of the Early Transmission of the Jesus Tradition." *Neotestamentica* 27 (1993) 205-31.

———. "Submission and Violence: Exploring Gender Relations in the First-Century World." *Neotestamentica* 34 (2000) 1-38.

Brant, Jo-Ann A. *Dialogue and Drama: Elements of Greek Tragedy in the Fourth Gospel*. Peabody, MA: Hendrickson, 2004.

Brison, Karen J. *Just Talk*. Berkeley: University of California Press, 1992.

Bibliography

Brogger, Jan, and David D. Gilmore. "The Matrifocal Family in Iberia: Spain and Portugal Compared." *Ethnology* 36 (1997) 13–30.

Brown, Raymond E. *The Gospel According to John*. 2 vols. Anchor Bible 29–29a. Garden City, NY: Doubleday, 1966–1970.

Bultmann, Rudolph. *The Gospel of John: A Commentary*. Philadelphia: Westminster, 1971.

Carson, Donald A. *The Gospel According to John*. Grand Rapids: Eerdmans, 1991.

Craffert, Pieter F. "Altered States of Consciousness: Visions, Spirit Possession, Sky Journeys." In *Understanding the Social World of the New Testament*, edited by Dietmar Neufeld and Richard E. DeMaris, 126–46. New York: Routledge, 2010.

———. *The Life of a Galilean Shaman: Jesus of Nazareth in Anthropological-Historical Perspective*. Matrix: The Bible in Mediterranean Context. Eugene, OR: Cascade, 2008.

Crook, Zeba A. "Honor, Shame, and Social Status Revisited." *Journal of Biblical Literature* 128 (2009) 591–611.

Culpepper, Alan. "Cognition in John: The Johannine Signs as Recognition Scenes." *Perspectives in Religious Studies* 35 (2008) 251–60.

———. *The Gospel and Letters of John*. Nashville: Abingdon, 1998.

Daniels, John W. "Gossip in the New Testament." *Biblical Theology Bulletin* 42 (2012) 204–13.

———. "Gossip in John's Gospel and the Social Processing of Jesus' Identity." *Journal of Early Christian History* 1 (2011) 9–29.

DeMaris, Richard E. "The Baptism of Jesus: A Ritual-Critical Approach." In *The Social Setting of Jesus and the Gospels*, edited by Wolfgang Stegemann et al., 137–57. Minneapolis: Fortress, 2002.

———. "Possession, Good and Bad—Ritual, Effects and Side-Effects: The Baptism of Jesus and Mark 1:9–11 From a Cross-Cultural Perspective." *Journal for the Study of the New Testament* 23 (2001) 3–29.

Draper, Jonathan A. *Orality, Literacy, and Colonialism in Antiquity*. Atlanta: Society of Biblical Literature, 2004.

Du Boulay, Juliet. *Portrait of a Greek Mountain Village*. Oxford Monographs on Social Anthropology. Oxford: Clarendon, 1974.

Dunn, James D. G. "Altering the Default Setting: Re-Envisaging the Early Transmission of the Jesus Tradition." *New Testament Studies* 49 (2003) 139–75.

Eliade, Mircea. *Shamanism: Archaic Techniques of Ecstacy*. Princeton: Princeton University Press, 1972.

Elliott, John H., and Dan O. Via. *What is Social-Scientific Criticism? Guides to Biblical Scholarship*. Minneapolis: Fortress, 1993.

Esler, Philip F. *Galatians*. New York: Routledge, 1998.

———. "Jesus and the Reduction of Intergroup Conflict." In *The Social Setting of Jesus and the Gospels*, edited by Wolfgang Stegemann et al., 185–205. Minneapolis: Fortress, 2002.

Bibliography

———. *Modelling Early Christianity: Social-Scientific Studies of the New Testament in Its Context.* New York: Routledge, 1995.

———. "Models in New Testament Interpretation: A Reply to David Horrell." *Journal for the Study of the New Testament* 78 (2000) 107–13.

Foster, Eric K. "Research on Gossip: Taxonomy, Methods, and Future Directions." *Review of General Psychology* 8 (2004) 78–99.

Foster, George M. "The Anatomy of Envy: A Study in Symbolic Behavior." *Current Anthropology* 13 (1972) 165–202.

———. "Interpersonal Relations in Peasant Society." *Human Organization* 19 (1960) 174–78.

———. "Peasant Society and the Image of Limited Good." *American Anthropologist* 67 (1965) 293–315.

Garrett, Susan R. "Sociology of Early Christianity." In *Anchor Bible Dictionary*, edited by David N. Freedman, 6:89–99. New York: Doubleday, 1992.

Geertz, Clifford. "'From the Native's Point of View': On the Nature of Anthropological Understanding." *Bulletin of the American Academy of Arts and Sciences* 28 (1974) 26–45.

Gilmore, David. *Aggression and Community.* New Haven: Yale University Press, 1987.

Gleason, Maud. "Visiting and News: Gossip and Reputation-Management in the Desert." *Journal of Early Christian Studies* 6 (1998) 501–21.

Gluckman, Max. "Gossip and Scandal." *Current Anthropology* 4 (1963) 307–16.

Gomes, Peter. "John 1:45–51." *Interpretation* 443 (1989) 282–86.

Greenwald, Anthony G., and Anthony R. Pratkanis. "The Self." In *The Handbook of Social Cognition.* Vol. 3, edited by Robert S. Wyler and Thomas K. Srull, 129–78. Hillsdale, NJ: Erlbaum, 1984.

Guss, David M. "The Enculturation of Makiritare Women." *Ethnology* 21 (1982) 259–69.

Halliday, M. A. K. "Anti-Languages." *American Anthropologist* 78 (1976) 570–84.

Handelman, Don. "Gossip in Encounters: The Transmission of Information in a Bounded Social Setting." *Man*, New Series, 8 (1973) 210–27.

Hanson, K. C., and Douglas E. Oakman. *Palestine in the Time of Jesus.* Minneapolis: Fortress, 1998.

Hearon, Holly. "The Interplay Between Written and Spoken Word in the Second Testament as Background to the Emergence of Written Gospels." *Oral Tradition* 25 (2010) 57–74.

Hebrew-English Edition of the Babylonian Talmud. Edited by Isedore Epstein. London: Soncino, 1965–1989.

Horrell, David G. "Models and Methods in Social-Scientific Interpretation: A Response to Philip Esler." *Journal for the Study of the New Testament* 78 (2000) 83–105.

Kartzow, Marianne B. "Female Gossipers and their Reputation in the Pastoral Epistles." *Neotestamentica* 39 (2005) 255–72.

Bibliography

———. *Gossip and Gender: Othering of Speech in the Pastoral Epistles*. Berlin: Walter de Gruyter, 2009.

Käsemann, Ernst. *The Testament of Jesus: A Study of the Gospel of John in the Light of Chapter 17*. Philadelphia: Fortress, 1968.

Keener, Craig S. *The Gospel of John: A Commentary*. 2 vols. Peabody, MA: Hendrickson, 2003.

Kelber, Werner H. "Modalities of Communication, Cognition and Physiology of Perception: Orality, Rhetoric, Scribality." *Semeia* 65 (1995) 194–215.

———. *The Oral and Written Gospel: The Hermeneutics of Speaking and Writing in the Synoptic Tradition, Mark, Paul, and Q*. Philadelphia: Fortress, 1983.

———. "Oral Tradition in Bible and New Testament Studies." *Oral Tradition* 18 (2003) 40–42.

———. "Orality and Biblical Studies: A Review Essay." *Review of Biblical Literature* 9 (2007) 1–25.

Kim, Stephen S. "The Christological and Eschatological Significance of Jesus' Miracle in John 5." *Bibliotheca Sacra* 165 (2008) 413–24.

———. "The Significance of Jesus' Raising Lazarus from the Dead in John 11." *Bibliotheca Sacra* 168 (2011) 53–62.

Koester, Craig R. "Messianic Exegesis and the Call of Nathanael (John 1.45–51)." *Journal for the Study of the New Testament* 12 (1990) 23–34.

Larsen, Kasper Bro. "Narrative Docetism: Christology and Storytelling in the Gospel of John." In *The Gospel of John and Christian Theology*, edited by Richard Bauckham and Carl Mosser, 346–55. Grand Rapids: Eerdmans, 2008.

———. *Recognizing the Stranger*. Leiden: Brill, 2008.

Lewis, Sian. *News and Society in the Greek Polis*. Chapel Hill: University of North Carolina Press, 1996.

Lucian. *Calumnia Non Temere Credendum*. Translated by A. M. Harmon et al. Loeb Classical Library. Cambridge: Harvard University Press, 1967–1976.

Malina, Bruce J. *Christian Origins and Cultural Anthropology: Practical Models for Biblical Interpretation*. Atlanta: John Knox, 1986.

———. "Collectivism in Mediterranean Culture." In *Understanding the Social World of the New Testament*, edited by Dietmar Neufeld and Richard E. DeMaris, 17–28. New York: Routledge, 2010.

———. "Early Christian Groups: Using Small Group Formation Theory to Explain Christian Organizations." In *Modelling Early Christianity: Social-Scientific Studies of the New Testament in its Context*, edited by Philip Esler, 92–109. New York: Routledge, 1995.

———. "Limited Good and the Social World of Early Christianity." *Biblical Theology Bulletin* 8 (1978) 162–76.

———. *The New Testament World: Insights from Cultural Anthropology*. Louisville: Westminster John Knox, 2001.

———. *The Social World of Jesus and the Gospels*. New York: Routledge, 1996.

Malina, Bruce J., and Jerome H. Neyrey. *Calling Jesus Names: The Social Value of Labels in Matthew*. Sonoma, CA: Polebridge, 1988.

Bibliography

———. *Portraits of Paul: An Archaeology of Ancient Personality.* Louisville: Westminster John Knox, 1996.

Malina, Bruce J., and John J. Pilch. *Social-Scientific Commentary on the Letters of Paul.* Minneapolis: Fortress, 1998.

Malina, Bruce J., and Richard L. Rohrbaugh. *Social-Science Commentary on the Gospel of John.* Minneapolis: Fortress, 1998.

———. *Social-Science Commentary on the Synoptic Gospels.* Minneapolis: Fortress, 2003.

Martin, Dale B. *Pedagogy of the Bible: An Analysis and Proposal.* Louisville: Westminster John Knox, 2008.

Meng, Margaret. "Gossip: Killing Us Softly." *Homiletic and Pastoral Review* 109 (2008) 26–31.

Merry, Sally E. "Rethinking Gossip and Scandal." In *Toward a General Theory of Social Control.* Vol. 1, *Fundamentals*, edited by Donald J. Black, 271–301. Orlando: Academic, 1984.

Milgram, Stanley, and Hans Toch. "Collective Behavior: Crowds and Social Movements." In *The Handbook of Social Psychology*, edited by Gardner Lindzey and Elliot Aronson, 1:507–610. Reading, MA: Addison-Wesley, 1969.

Moloney, Francis J. *The Gospel of John.* Sacra Pagina 4. Collegeville, MN: Liturgical, 1998.

Neyrey, Jerome H. *The Gospel of John.* Cambridge: Cambridge University Press, 2007.

———. "Group Orientation." In *Handbook of Biblical Social Values*, edited by John J. Pilch and Bruce J. Malina, 94–98. Peabody, MA: Hendrickson, 1998.

———. "'I Am the Door' (John 10:7, 9): Jesus as Broker in the Fourth Gospel." *Catholic Biblical Quarterly* 69 (2007) 271–91.

———. "Limited Good." In *Handbook of Biblical Social Values*, edited by John J. Pilch and Bruce J. Malina, 122–27. Peabody, MA: Hendrickson, 1998.

———. "The 'Noble Shepherd' in John 10: Cultural and Rhetorical Background." *Journal of Biblical Literature* 120 (2001) 267–91.

———. *Paul in Other Words: A Cultural Reading of His Letters.* Louisville: Westminster John Knox, 1990.

Neyrey, Jerome H., and Richard L. Rohrbaugh. "'He Must Increase, I Must Decrease' (John 3:30): A Cultural and Social Interpretation." In *The Social World of the New Testament*, edited by Jerome H. Neyrey and Eric C. Stewart, 235–54. Grand Rapids: Baker, 2008.

O'Day, Gail R. *Revelation in the Fourth Gospel: Narrative Mode and Theological Claim.* Philadelphia: Fortress, 1986.

———. *The Word Disclosed: Preaching the Gospel of John.* St. Louis: Chalice, 2002.

O'Neill, J. C. "Son of Man, Stone of Blood (John 1:51)." *Novum Testamentum* 55 (2003) 374–81.

Bibliography

Ong, Walter J. *The Presence of the Word: Some Prolegomena for Cultural and Religious History*. New Haven: Yale University Press, 1967.

Paine, Robert. "What is Gossip? An Alternative Hypothesis." *Man*, New Series, 2 (1967) 278–85.

Pilch, John J. "Altered States of Consciousness in the Synoptics." In *The Social Setting of Jesus and the Gospels*, edited by Wolfgang Stegemann et al., 103–16. Minneapolis: Fortress, 2002.

———. "Are there Jews and Christians in the Bible?" *HTS Teolgiese Studies* 53 (1997) 119–25.

———. *Flights of the Soul: Visions, Heavenly Journeys, and Peak Experiences in the Biblical World*. Grand Rapids: Eerdmans, 2011.

———. *Healing in the New Testament*. Minneapolis: Fortress, 2000.

———. "Purity." In *Handbook of Biblical Social Values*, edited by John J. Pilch and Bruce J. Malina, 170–73. Peabody, MA: Hendrickson, 1998.

———. "Secrecy in the Mediterranean World: An Anthropological Perspective." *Biblical Theology Bulletin* 24 (1994) 151–57.

Pitt-Rivers, Julian. "Honour and Social Status." In *Honour and Shame: The Values of Mediterranean Society*, edited by Jean G. Peristiany, 21–77. Chicago: University of Chicago Press, 1966.

Plutarch. *Moralia*. Translated by F. C. Babbit and William Helmbold et al. Loeb Classical Library. Cambridge: Harvard University Press, 1969.

Rhoads, David. "Performance Criticism: An Emerging Methodology in the Second Testament—Part 1." *Biblical Theology Bulletin* 36 (2006) 118–34.

———. "Performance Criticism: An Emerging Methodology in the Second Testament—Part 2." *Biblical Theology Bulletin* 36 (2006) 164–85.

Rohrbaugh, Richard L. "Honor: Core Value in the Biblical World." In *Understanding the Social World of the New Testament*, edited by Dietmar Neufeld and Richard E. DeMaris, 109–25. New York: Routledge, 2010.

———. *The New Testament in Cross-Cultural Perspective*. Matrix: The Bible in Mediterranean Context. Eugene, OR: Cascade, 2007.

Rosnow, Ralph L., and Gary A. Fine. *Rumor and Gossip: The Social Psychology of Hearsay*. New York: Elsevier, 1976.

Rysman, Alexander. "How the 'Gossip' Became a Woman." *Journal of Communication* 27 (1977) 176–80.

Schnackenburg, Rudolph. *The Gospel of John*. 3 vols. New York: Crossroad, 1980–1982.

Sedler, M. D. *Stop the Runaway Conversation: Take Control over Gossip and Criticism*. Grand Rapids: Chosen, 2001.

Smith, D. Moody. *John*. Abingdon New Testament Commentaries. Nashville: Abingdon, 1999.

Smith, Morton. *Jesus the Magician*. San Francisco: Harper & Row, 1978.

Stewart, Eric C. *Gathered Around Jesus: An Alternative Spatial Practice in the Gospel of Mark*. Matrix: The Bible in Mediterranean Context. Eugene, OR: Cascade, 2009.

Bibliography

———. "Social Stratification and Patronage in Ancient Mediterranean Societies." In *Understanding the Social World of the New Testament*, edited by Dietmar Neufeld and Richard E. DeMaris, 156–66. New York: Routledge, 2010.

Strecker, Christian. "Jesus and the Demoniacs." In *The Social Setting of Jesus and the Gospels*, edited by Wolfgang Stegemann et al., 117–33. Minneapolis: Fortress, 2002.

Tacitus. *Annals and the Histories*. Edited by Moses Hadas. New York: Modern Library, 2003.

Talbert, Charles H. *Reading John: A Literary and Theological Commentary on the Fourth Gospel and the Johannine Epistles*. New York: Crossroad, 1992.

Triandis, Harry C. "An Etic-Emic Analysis of Individualism and Collectivism." *Journal of Cross-Cultural Psychology* 24 (1993) 366–83.

———. *Individualism and Collectivism*. San Francisco: Westview, 1995.

Van Eck, Ernest. "Invitations and Excuses that are not Invitations and Excuses: Gossip in Luke 14:18–20." *HTS Teolgiese Studies* 68 (2012).

Yerkovich, Sally. "Gossiping as a Way of Speaking." *Journal of Communication* 27 (1977) 192–97.

www.ingramcontent.com/pod-product-compliance
Lightning Source LLC
Chambersburg PA
CBHW071624170426
43195CB00038B/2111